FIREFLY

GUIDE TO
DESERTS

ANDREW WARREN & TONY ALLAN, GENERAL EDITORS

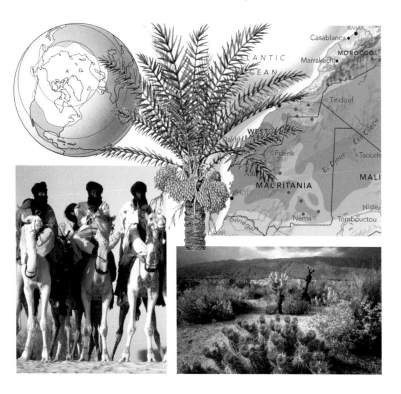

FIREFLY BOOKS

A FIREFLY BOOK

Published by Firefly Books Ltd. 2006

First printing

Publisher Cataloging-in-Publication Data (U.S.)

Guide to deserts / general editors Andrew Warren ;
Tony Allan.
[208] p. : col. photos. ; cm.
Includes index.
Summary: A comprehensive review of the
world's deserts with maps of arid regions.
Includes detailed information about flora and
fauna, people living on the desert margins,
and conservation tactics and resources.
ISBN-13: 978-1-55407-213-2 (pbk.)
ISBN-10: 1-55407-213-1 (pbk.)
1. Deserts. 2. Desert ecology. I. Allan,
J. A. (John Anthony). II. Warren, Andrew. III. Title.
508.315/4 dc22   GB611.G83 2006

Library and Archives Canada Cataloguing in
Publication

Guide to deserts / general editors, Andrew Warren
and Tony Allan. Includes index.
ISBN-13: 978-1-55407-213-2
ISBN-10: 1-55407-213-1
1. Deserts. I. Allan, J. A. (John Anthony)
II. Warren, Andrew
GB611.G83 2006   909.0954   C2006-902044-2

Published in the United States by
Firefly Books (U.S.) Inc.
P.O. Box 1338, Ellicott Station
Buffalo, New York 14205

Published in Canada by
Firefly Books Ltd.
66 Leek Crescent
Richmond Hill, Ontario L4B 1H1

GENERAL EDITORS Andrew Warren, Tony Allan

COMMISSIONING EDITOR Steve Luck

EDITOR Cathy Lowne

EXECUTIVE ART EDITOR Mike Brown

DESIGNER Caroline Ohara

PRODUCTION Åsa Sonden

FRONT COVER : t/ Ice sheets, Philip's;
tc Date palm, Philip's; tr Sahara desert
map, Philip's; b/ Tuareg tribesmen,
Corbis; br Flowering cacti, Corbis;
BACK COVER : Rock weathering, Philip's;
Scorpion, Philip's;

Printed in China

CONTENTS

FOREWORD

The world's hot deserts, covering around 25 per cent of its land surface, conjure up many emotions and many contradictory ideas—hardship and romance, barrenness, and awe-inspiring beauty.

The driest places on Earth, deserts are home to 350 million people and some of the rarest and most curious species of plants and animals known. Culturally and spiritually they stand in the center of at least two of the great religions. The desert was the backdrop to the life and teachings of the Prophet Muhammad, while Jesus was tempted by the devil in one such wilderness.

For some, deserts mean black gold: half of the world's oil comes from them and three-quarters of oil reserves lie beneath their sands. For others they offer the opportunity of a low carbon—or even carbon-free—world, controlling climate change. Makers of solar power plants claim there is enough solar radiation hitting just one percent of their surface to meet the whole world's needs.

Life in deserts

Desert ecosystems support the growing understanding that the environment is not a luxury, but a key factor in overcoming poverty and an economic basis for livelihoods, true sustainable development.

Their often harsh and arid conditions have spawned animals and plants uniquely adapted to them. Flora in a variety of fantastical forms—sometimes able to lie dormant for years —burst into short-lived but highly productive life after rain.

Such super fast growth and massive seed production—so essential for survival—has made many dryland plants the basis of agricultural societies. Wheat and barley evolved from desert annuals in the Near East some 7,000–9,000 years ago as did maize and squash in southern Mexico around 4000 BCE. Experts believe other food crops are waiting to be discovered in these unique natural laboratories.

Chemicals and pharmaceuticals, derived from micro-algae and medicinal plants that thrive in the year-round high solar radiation, are emerging onto global markets: many scientists suspect that, given the unique evolutionary history of many desert plants, their real pharmaceutical potential has yet to be realized.

Romantic deserts

The romance of the desert—fueled by such classic literature as *The Thousand and One Nights* and movies like *Lawrence of Arabia*—increasingly attracts tourists. Tourism can be a damaging extractive industry, consuming and subsuming the environment and cultures it visits. But sensitively managed, it can deliver sustainable livelihoods and a new generation of fans of the desert world.

I am sure that this excellent book will stimulate interest across the world among young and old, in desert countries and beyond, helping current and new generations to marvel and fascinate over these unique places and landscapes.

UNEP is proud to have worked with Andrew Warren, one of the book's authors, on our recently published Global Deserts Outlook. Governments have asked UNEP to keep the state of the world's environment under assessment. Deserts, possibly the Cinderella of the globe's ecosystems, are finally and deservedly being brought into the spotlight.

International Year of Deserts

The book is also fittingly being published in the United Nations International Year of Deserts and Desertification.

Let us hope that the Year and the book can help bring greater clarity to these two separate but related issues.

While deserts are unique ecosystems in their own right, desertification is one of the hardest and most intractable environmental problems. Some 36 countries are affected by it or by land degradation in Africa alone, and an estimated 75 percent of the continent's farmland is rapidly losing the basic nutrients needed to grow crops. Some estimate the cost of this loss—in some of the poorest countries on Earth—as $4 billion a year.

Poverty is a primary driving force behind the process. It forces many farmers to cultivate marginal land continuously, without fallow periods, thus crippling it. We must urgently break this cycle by offering alternative livelihoods and regaining traditional land management and wisdom—and through direct measures like promoting agroforestry and harnessing the abilities of earth worms, beetles, fungi bacteria, and other organisms to boost the fertility of the soil.

Without such management, the desert margins—where the drylands and the desert lands meet—will continue to witness an unsustainable battle, with tragic long term consequences for both their ecosystems and their peoples.

Achim Steiner,
Executive Director of the United Nations
Environment Programme (UNEP), 2006

WHAT ARE DESERTS?

Deserts have become much more familiar to most of us in the last few years. There may be some people who still imagine them to be dune-covered wastes, inhabited by romantic Bedouin, but those who live in them have little difficulty in contradicting these quaint fancies. So, too, can most of the people who do not live in deserts, having either visited them or seen real deserts on the media. They all know that there are large, fully functioning cities, highways, airports, hotels and hospitals in parts of the desert, and that some of the world's richest people come from or live in the desert.

In plain English, a "desert" is a deserted place, so how can it be that some deserts support cities with more than five million people? The contradiction arises because another meaning of the word "desert" has crept into common usage. To most people, "desert" now means "a very dry place." Better scientific terms are "hyperarid and arid lands." The slippage in the common meaning is not hard to understand, and not the total contradiction that it may at first seem: almost all very dry places were, until recently, deserted or nearly so, and a glance at the now well-known satellite image of the world at night will tell you that most dry places are even yet deserted. The hotels and highways have invaded only a very small corner of the vast dry spaces on the planet.

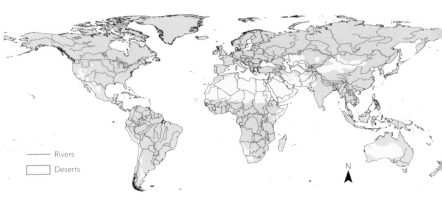

Rivers

Deserts

N
▲

▲ *The relationship between deserts and rivers is complex. Surprisingly, some of the largest rivers in the world such as the Nile, the Indus, and the Colorado all flow through desert regions.*

Deserts can be defined in many ways, which nevertheless all pick out the same core deserts and disagree only about their margins. Now that we have good satellite imagery of the whole world, the simplest, and probably the best way is to define deserts is by the cover of vegetation: quite simply, places with little vegetation are deserts. The map derived from satellite images can be compared with earlier attempts to define the desert using climatic data (for rainfall and evaporation) with an "aridity index." There are problems with both of these definitions. There are some polar areas with little vegetation, for example. There is a good argument for calling these places "deserts" not least because many of them have very little rain or snowfall. An easy compromise is to call them "cold deserts" to distinguish them from the common understanding, which is that "deserts" are hot, at least at one season. The climatic definition suffers problems too, the main one being that climatic stations are very few in deserts. Despite these problems, it is

▶ *One common definition of deserts describes them as places lacking in vegetation. This enhanced satellite image clearly shows the sparse desert regions of North Africa and the Middle East, Central Asia, southern Africa, Australia and smaller, but noticeable, the desert regions of North and South America.*

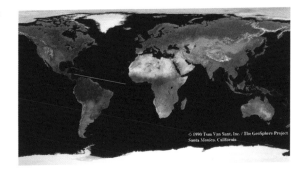

© 1990 Tom Van Sant, Inc. / The GeoSphere Project
Santa Monica, California

reassuring to see that "deserts" come out in much the same place, whether defined by vegetation cover or by an aridity index. In other words, and rather obviously, vegetation does not grow in deserts because there is little water.

Desert rain

The climatic data do, however, allow us to make more precise generalizations about the climates of these dry, unvegetated places. Not only is there very little rain, the rain that does come is very unpredictable. Deserts that are north or south of subtropics have more of what little rain they get in

Desert formation

Where rain is infrequent but heavy, it cuts deep, steep-sided valleys called *wadis* (1), which isolate buttes (2) and the larger mesas (3). The steep-sided valleys have been excavated over millions of years by occasional floods. Rocky surfaces are much more common than sand seas in the desert. About 30% of Arabian deserts are sand covered, whereas only 1% of desert surface in North America is sandy. Some of the rain that falls on the mountains may drain into porous rock layers (4) that can stretch many kilometres beneath the desert. Wherever these porous layers meet the surface, a spring is formed and may feed an oasis (5). Finding and utilizing water is the most urgent problem in the desert, and one ancient solution that is still used is the *qanat* (6). First a head well (7) is sunk down to the porous deposits, which may be 330 ft (100 m) deep. Then a line of ventilation shafts (8) is dug, and finally a channel (9) is begun from the *qanat* mouth (10). When the *qanat* is completed, gravity brings the water to the settlement, and canals (11) take it where it is needed.

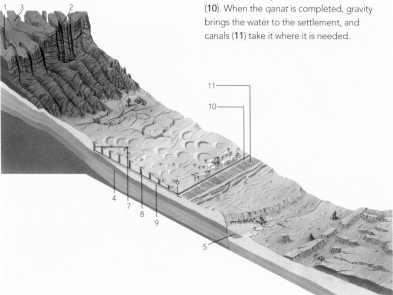

winter, as many travelers' tales attest, and deserts nearer the Equator a little more of their sparse rain in summer, when they are reached by the tail ends of the monsoons. The hyperarid deserts (most of them between these two zones) have no real seasonal pattern of rainfall. In the extreme deserts, as in the central Sahara or in northern Chile, it may not rain for years. When the rain comes, it is often intense. The entire rainfall for years may come in a few hours. These storms can be very local—in other words they are "spotty". One place may be drenched, but at the same time, another place a few miles away will be bone dry. In the cold deserts, like the Gobi, there can be snowfall in winter.

Most deserts, especially those in the interiors of continents, and even those in northern Central Asia, have very high summer temperatures. Most also have great daily ranges of temperature, for deserts lack a cloud cover that at night would act to keep in warmth. Common daily temperature variations are 36°F (20°C). Some mid-latitude continental deserts—even the northern Sahara— have frequent nighttime frosts in winter.

Desert landscapes

It takes much more than aridity to create a desert landscape. At the largest of scales, geological history provides the broad framework. The biggest of the tropical deserts, in the Sahara, southern Africa and Australia are "shield deserts": pieces of an ancient, hard, much-eroded "super-continent," known as Gondwana, which broke up between 100 and 200 million years ago. The shield deserts are wide, gently undulating plains, with a few isolated hills of harder rock, like Uluru in Australia. The plains have been gently flexed into very gently sloping swells and basins. Most of the basins have been filled slowly, over many millions of years, with sediments, some of which hold oil deposits, and almost all of which hold valuable water. Here and there, more recent intrusions of volcanic rock have created highlands in the shield deserts, like those of Tibesti and the Ahaggar in the Sahara.

▼ *The popular image that deserts are all huge expanses of sand is wrong. Despite harsh conditions, deserts contain some of the most varied landscapes in the world. They are also one of the most extensive environments—the hot*

Erg

Reg

Desert mountains

and cold deserts together cover almost 40% of the Earth's surface.

The three types of hot desert are known by their Arabic names: sand desert, called erg, covers only about a quarter of the world's desert; the rest is divided between mountains (usually of bare rock) and reg (broad plains covered by loose gravel or pebbles).

In areas of erg, such as parts of the Namib Desert, the shape of the dunes reflects the character of local winds. Where winds are constant in direction, crescent-shaped barchan dunes form. In areas of bare rock, wind-blown sand is a major agent of erosion.

Mountain-and-basin deserts are very different. These are deserts in more recently active parts of the Earth's crust, where folding and faulting have created jagged mountain ranges, with plains between. The mountains are cut deeply by river valleys, into which huge landslides sometimes intrude, triggered by earthquakes. The deserts of North and South America and of Central Asia fall into this category. In Asia, the glaciers and snows in the high mountains feed huge rivers that flow across these deserts, like the Amudarya and Syrdarya, the Indus and (formerly) the Tarim.

Formed by rivers

Surface process put some finishing details onto the geological framework. Rivers are the most important of these processes, shaping the greater part of the desert landscape, even if they run only occasionally. There are many wide pebble-covered plateaus in the shield deserts, where rivers have very rarely flowed, yet even here one can find the occasional gully. In the mountains, the rivers have cut valleys, some of them very deep, out of which they have carried debris to the plains, where they have deposited it as broad spreads, fanning out from their exits from the mountains. Lakes collect in some of the huge basins of the shield deserts, which are usually dry, and the narrower basins of the mountain-and-basin deserts, building up salt and clay deposits. About one quarter of the desert is covered by sand, shaped by the wind into dunes; the wind has also cut into hard rocks in places, creating aerodynamic corridors or small hillocks.

Plants add even finer details. With little water, vegetation is sparse, and in much of the Sahara and Arabia, and parts of northern Chile, almost completely absent. Many plants are adapted to take opportunistic advantage of sporadic rainfall by germinating from seed, growing, and flowering very quickly after a rainstorm. Others, such as cacti, are slow growing but efficient at moisture retention. Vegetation is dense only where there are sources of moisture, such as the sandy beds of ephemeral streams, or around springs. In these places moisture and intense sunlight can create very lush oases.

Although deserts are considered inhospitable, around 13 percent of the world's population live there. The hyperarid cores are virtually uninhabited, and the greatest density of population lives near to the great rivers.

These clarifications do not get us away from more questions: why are deserts so dry? Why are some places dry and others wet? Have deserts, as dry places, always been dry? Will they continue to be dry, or will other places become deserts?

WHY ARE THERE DESERTS?

The deserts lie on the globe in the places where rainfall is naturally low, or where temperatures are high enough to evaporate whatever water there is. These dry areas are the result of one or more of four factors: atmospheric high-pressure zones, "continentality," cold ocean currents and "rain-shadows."

Atmospheric high-pressure zones

The biggest deserts lie around the 30°S and the 30°N latitudes. The Sahara, the Arabian deserts, the Kalahari and the Australian deserts are in this category. Subtropical high-pressure zones are responsible for their dryness.

The global distribution of land and ocean ensures that the high-pressure belts do not form continuous bands around the globe. In the Americas and in southeast Asia, moist air from the small seas fends off the subtropical high-pressure zones, and the huge dry areas beneath them, even if these areas are at the same latitudes as the deserts in Africa and Australia.

Continentality

North or south of the zone of subtropical highs on the globe, the generally westerly winds lose their moisture to the coasts of the continents, and are desiccated before they reach their interiors, where, therefore, there are more deserts, as in Central Asia and western North America. The wet monsoons coming from the east into India and China are desiccated in this way before they reach into the Chinese and Indian deserts. The Taklimakan Desert of western China is the only hyperarid desert outside the subtropical high-pressure zones.

Cold ocean currents

The third cause of deserts is cold oceanic currents moving from the poles toward the tropics along the western coasts of the continents, or the upwelling of cold water far from the poles. The surfaces of cool seas have lower rates of evaporation from their surface than warmer seas. Examples of these cool currents are the Benguela Current along the southwest coast of Africa, which affects the Namib Desert, the Peru Current along the west coast of South America, further drying the Atacama Desert, and the cool upwelling current near to the Omani coast in eastern Arabia. These hyperarid coastal strips are frequently engulfed in fog, which is created when cold sea meets warm air. In these areas, moisture is delivered more by fog than by rain. The fogs and sea breezes greatly moderate air temperatures, so that these hyperarid deserts have quite moderate temperatures.

Rain shadows

Dryness is intensified in deserts that are sheltered from the prevailing wind by a mountain range. The downwind desert is said to be in a "rain shadow": as air masses move up and over the mountains, moisture develops into clouds and falls as rain. On the other side of the range, the subsiding air is extremely dry. There are examples of this kind of desert in western North America (east of the Sierra Nevada and other smaller mountain ranges, and in the Monte Desert and Patagonia in Argentina (east of the Andes). There are other examples in Central Asia, where aridity, already caused by continentality, is enhanced by descending, dry air.

Classifying desert climates

Deserts can be divided according to their rainfall conditions: some seldom receive rain or experience fog instead of rain, others have either a winter or a summer rainy season, or even two rainy seasons. Temperature is also a useful means of classification. Some deserts are hot during the day all year, some have a great annual range of temperature, and others are cool and have cold winters. Scientists estimate that 43 percent of arid lands are hot desert, with average summer temperatures above 86°F (30°C), while 24 percent are cold deserts, with average winter temperatures below 32°F (0°C).

The Hadley Cell

The high-pressure zones responsible for desert aridity are themselves the result of a convection pattern called the Hadley Cell. Because the Sun's radiation is greatest near the Equator, air there is heated and so rises, creating low-pressure zones at the surface (**1**). Moisture-bearing air masses are then sucked into these zones, bringing the intense rainfall that supports the rainforests (**2**). At high altitude, the equatorial air masses then move a few degrees in latitude toward the poles, and slowly subside as they cool (**3**). As the air descends, it becomes drier and creates high pressure. These high-pressure cells, or "anticyclones," are known as "the subtropical highs." The high pressure blocks the incursion of moist air. At or near the surface, the air circulates back to the Equator (**4**), creating the Trade Winds over the oceans, and dusty desert winds known as the *Harmattan* over West Africa.

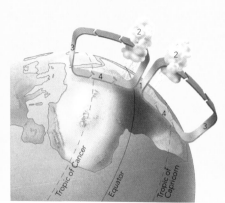

CLIMATE

Deserts are not all barren, windswept, sandy expanses where rain never falls. In fact, although all deserts are short of water, they exhibit a great range of climates. Scientific explanation of aridity concerns a variety of atmospheric processes based on such things as subtropical high-pressure cells, continental winds, land forms and ocean currents. At any particular location, these combine to cause a particular climate regime.

Types of climate

Deserts have an immense range of air temperatures. In the Sahara, Arabian Peninsula, Sonoran Desert of California, Australian deserts and Kalahari, the anticyclonic (high-pressure) weather systems bring clear skies with high ground temperatures and a marked cooling at night. In tropical areas, like Somalia, there is little change in monthly temperatures. By contrast, deserts in continental interiors—notably the arid areas of Asia and the western United States—have large seasonal temperature ranges, with very cold winters and very hot summers. The Iranian, Nevada and Gobi deserts are sometimes described as having "temperate" climates because of their cold winters.

On the leeward sides of mountain ranges, such as the Sierra Nevada, the Great Dividing Range in Australia and the Andes, extremely arid conditions prevail. Most rain that falls from moisture-bearing winds does so on the mountains, and so there is a "rain shadow" effect.

Deserts that have clear skies, as most do, receive large amounts of energy from the sun. The high reflectivity of sand and rocks reduces the effects of this energy on the ground, but is not sufficient to prevent significant evaporation of water and heating of the air. At night, the clear skies allow rapid heat loss from both ground and air.

Wind speeds are not necessarily higher in arid lands. Indeed, because stable air masses are dominant, winds are often light. However, localized surface heating can produce high local wind velocities, as in dust devils.

Climatic change

We all know that the weather is not constant, and when the Swiss-born geologist Louis Agassiz, in the 1840s, drew attention to the evidence that there had been an ice age in the recent geological past, scientists had to concede that neither was climate. We now have very much more evidence of climatic

▶ *About 20,000 years ago (1) permanent ice sheets covered 16 million sq mi (42 million km²) compared with the present 6 million sq mi (15 million km²) (2). Large ice sheets can result in less global rainfall, and bring about an expansion of arid regions.*

▼ **The Earth's** *climatic regions.*

Tropical climate (hot with rain all year)

Desert climate (hot and very dry)

Savanna climate (hot with dry season)

Steppe climate (warm and dry)

Mild climate (warm and wet)

Continental climate (wet with cold winter)

Subarctic climate (very cold winter)

Polar climate (very cold and dry)

Mountainous climate (altitude affects climate)

fluctuations in the past, and immensely better ways of dating the geological record they left behind. It cannot now be doubted that Earth's climate has fluctuated significantly over both short and long periods, even after *Homo sapiens* evolved, and even after the last glaciers left northwestern Europe and the northern United States. Like the glaciers, the deserts waxed and waned.

It is now believed that there have been at least ten major glacial cycles, or ice ages, in the last one and a half million years (depending on one's definition of "major cycle"). The last one was at its height 20–18,000 years ago. Drastic changes occurred in the Earth's climatic systems during each glacial cycle. Much more water was stored in ice and much less in the oceans during the ice ages. Temperatures during the last glacial were on average 5°C (9°F) less than they are today in the atmosphere and 4–5°F (2–3°C) less on the surfaces of the oceans. The cool temperatures and the decrease in surface area of the oceans meant that there was less evaporation from the ocean surface, and this contributed to a reduction in rainfall and the expansion of the deserts.

Wet-dry climate swings

Just as the deserts expanded in the cold periods, they contracted when the Earth warmed again. Higher sea levels and higher temperatures encouraged more evaporation from the oceans, which in turn fed more moisture to the winds that moved over the continents, which then brought more rain than now to many of the deserts. These wet-dry swings occurred from the start of the glacial era, but we know less of the earlier changes than the later ones.

For periods even shorter than those properly called climatic changes, other changes are labelled "desiccation" if they last a decade or so; and "drought" if they last no more than a few years. It is not unusual for rainfall to vary by more than 50 percent from year to year. In parts of Sudan annual rainfall from 1965 to 1985 was 40 percent less than from 1920 to 1940. In places that depend so utterly on rainfall, these can be life-changing events, as they were in the Sudan and in the rest of the African Sahel in the 1970s and 1980s.

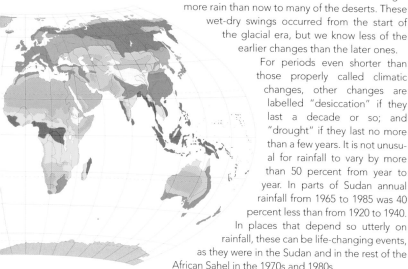

The changes of climate of the last few thousand years were not at all unusual in geological time. There are thought to be at least two reasons why global climatic should change (at this scale). The first is a complex set of cycles in the Earth's orbit round the Sun, the angle of its tilt, and the way its tilt rotates, known as the "Milankovitch cycles," named after a Serbian astronomer who proposed the theory. The cycles control the amount, seasonal, and global distribution of the Sun's input of heat to the Earth's atmosphere. The second process that influences climate is the distribution of oceans and continents, itself controlled by continental drift. In some geological periods there were huge continents, in whose interiors continentality ensured very little rain. The distribution of the continents also determines the course of both the oceanic currents that take warm, moist air toward some places, and the cool currents that help to create some modern deserts. For all these changes, the deserts of the past, like those of today, were generally in the subtropics, and the reasons for their existence were the same. The movement of the continents, however, means that ancient desert rocks are today found almost anywhere on Earth, as they have been in northern Canada, or in the Midlands of England.

Deserts in the rock record

The record of the past is incomplete because it has been eroded, or because it has been altered out of recognition by rock metamorphism, or because it is now buried very deeply. Nonetheless there are many places where it has been preserved and is accessible. It is these remnants that we use to infer the existence and character of the ancient deserts. The most useful rocks in this regard are sedimentary, and sedimentologists go through a sequence of analyzing them that is something like this: they believe that their sandstone (for example) was once a sand dune (or a river deposit); they then examine the way in which modern sand dunes (or river

▼ **The geological timescale** is a way of categorizing periods of time since the formation of the Earth 4,600 million years ago. The longest divisions of time are known as the four great eras, each of which is broken down into periods, and in the case of the most recent era, the Cenozoic, into epochs. The table was devised by studying the correlation of rock formations, fossils, and radiometric dating.

GEOLOGICAL TIMESCALE

Precambrian	Lower		Palaeozoic (Primary)			Upper				Mesozoic (Secondary)				Cenozoic (Tertiary, Quaternary)						Era
Precambrian	Cambrian	Ordovician	Silurian	Devonian	Carboniferous		Permian	Triassic	Jurassic	Cretaceous		Palaeocene	Eocene	Oligocene	Miocene	Pliocene	Pleistocene			System
			CALEDONIAN FOLDING		HERCYNIAN FOLDING					LARAMIDE FOLDING	ALPINE FOLDING									Orogeny

600   550   500   450   400   350   300   250   200   150   100   50

Millions of years before present

deposits) are "bedded" in thin or thick layers and the sizes and surface textures of their sands. They need as large a repertoire of these modern deposits as possible. They then measure these same characteristics in the ancient rocks. They should then be able to infer the kinds of dune (or desert river) that created the ancient rock, and the direction and strength of the winds (or rivers) that built it. We now know, for example the directions of the winds that created the dune rocks that outcrop in central England, Greenland, and the Grand Canyon, and the directions of the desert rivers that created the Old Red Sandstone of Devon, and may other places.

More than that, these ancient desert sediments help geologists to reconstruct the ways in which the continents moved, divided, and collided over geological time. The New Red Sandstones of the Midlands and northeast of England, for example, show us that they were formed closer to the Equator than they now are. Ancient desert flood deposits and evaporites, containing high salt concentrations, have also been identified, sometimes in close association with ancient dune sands, as in the case of the Rotliegend Desert rocks of the North Sea basin, which date from the early Permian period (about 290 million years ago). Continental drift created other anomalies in today's deserts. In the middle of the Sahara, and in parts of Oman, there are glacial deposits (moraines and striations) that were formed when the rocks were near the South Pole in the Permo-Carboniferous period (about 290 million years ago).

The desert rocks of the Rotliegend under the North Sea are now well known largely because they, like many other ancient dune sandstones, hold large quantities of oil and gas in their open porous structures. The ancient dune sands of Colorado and Wyoming, the Cooper Basin of South Australia, and northwest Europe are other important examples of ancient desert sediments that are now major sources of oil and gas.

Deserts in the Quaternary period

For the Quaternary Period (from about 1.5 million years ago), and especially for the last few tens of thousands of years, we have yet more tools to break into geological history. The dating tools that are used for more ancient geological periods are neither as accurate nor as easy to apply. Some 50 years ago Quaternary history was blown open with carbon 14 dating. The method, however, took history only to some 5,000 years ago, and was of little use in dating most desert sediments, in which there is little carbon. Optically Stimulated Luminescence (OSL) became possible about 30 years ago, and not only does it work best on the sandy and loessic sediments (wind-blown dust deposits) of the dry lands, but may be able to date sediments that are 500,000 years old. It has re-opened the history of deserts.

The second set of tools with which the Quaternary can be interpreted, and which can be applied only rarely to earlier geological periods, is the analysis of the landforms that were formed at that time, and survive on the surface. The glacial landforms of the Upper Quaternary were what gave Agassiz his ideas about the ice ages. The desert equivalents are ancient sand dunes, lakeshores, and river channels.

Ancient deserts

With these tools, we can now say that the last ice age was very dry in the deserts. Ancient sand seas, whose dunes are now fixed by grasses and bushes, and some of which are even cultivated, surround them all. These deposits show that the deserts were probably twice as extensive as they are today, and may have been even larger, in some parts of the Quaternary. Far from today's deserts, there were large, active fields of dunes in northern Europe, the Great Plains of North America, and Tasmania. Huge clouds of dust from the deserts and glacial outwash buried large parts of the Midwest of the United States, northern Europe, Russia and the Ukraine, China, northern Pakistan, and Argentina in loess (wind-blown dust deposits), now the parent material of some of the world's most productive soils.

Of more interest to historians and pre-historians is the evidence that there was a series of shorter wet and dry periods more recently still, almost up to the historical period. For example, we know that about 6,000 years ago, Lake Chad was a huge freshwater lake, bigger than the Caspian Sea is today. A Neolithic canoe has been excavated from a high shoreline of "Mega-Chad" in Nigeria. We also know that the lake was even larger in periods before that (perhaps in the last interglacial and probably before). There were other lakes, though none as big, in northwestern Sudan, northern Mali, and Libya (though some of them date back further into the Quaternary). The lake sediments of "Mega-Chad" are full of fossil crocodiles, whose descendants survive, stranded in pools in the nearby Ennedi Mountains. All across the Sahara, archaeological remains—including rock paintings—and ancient pollen show that the great lakes were accompanied by savanna vegetation, and that they supported large populations of humans. As to the dry periods between the wet ones, deep-sea cores show that there was a sharp decrease in rainfall, and an increase in dustiness about 4,200 years ago, which coincided with the ending of

► *Lake Chad* was *once a vast inland sea, which around 6,000 years ago, covered an estimated 150,000 sq mi (400,000 km²). With a surface area now of less than 550 sq mi (1,500 km²), it is feared that the lake could disappear altogether during the 21st century.*

the Akkadian Empire in Mesopotamia and of the Indus Valley Civilization in Pakistan and India. In North America, the dunes in the Nebraska Sand Hills became active more than once after the ice retreated, before being pinned down by grasses, as they now are.

There is no reason to believe that we have reached the end of climatic history. Changes like the ones that destroyed civilizations 4,000 years ago, are almost certain to occur again, but we still do not have a good idea of exactly when. Much more worrying is the strong evidence that we are experiencing climate change caused by our increasing input of carbon dioxide (and some other gasses) into the atmosphere. Temperatures have been rising more steeply in the last few years than ever before in the available climatic record, and probably for long before. Hotter conditions inevitably mean more evaporation and transpiration, and therefore drier conditions. Climate models show that this may not affect many deserts, as they are already very dry, but some deserts, particularly those in southern Africa may expand into areas now only semiarid. Deserts that depend on glacier- or snow-melt (southwestern USA, deserts around the Andes, and all the central Asian deserts) will suffer the most, because of the retreat and then disappearance of glaciers. Some models show the Sahelian fringe of the Sahara getting wetter, but rather slowly if at all.

WATER IN THE DESERT

Deserts, surprisingly, contain some of the world's largest rivers, such as the Colorado in the USA, the Indus, Tigris and Euphrates, Tarim and Amudarya and Syrdarya in Asia, and the Nile and Niger in Africa. These rivers are known as "exogenous," because their sources lie outside the arid zone. They are vital for sustaining life in some of the driest parts of the world. For centuries, the annual floods of the Nile, Tigris, and Euphrates brought fertile silts and water to the inhabitants of their lower valleys. Today, river discharges are increasingly controlled by dams and barrages, many of which impound water that crosses international borders and so lead to international disputes. There are many examples: the Colorado River flows from the USA to Mexico; the Tigris and Euphrates flow from Turkey through Syria to Iraq; the Indus and its tributaries share their water between India and Pakistan; and the rivers that flow from, to, and between the complex jigsaw of new countries in former Soviet central Asia. The Tarim River has not flowed beyond the great oases of western China since 1972.

The flow of exogenous rivers varies with the season. On the plains they rise several months after rain has fallen in the mountains, or after the glaciers and snows have melted. Peak flow in the desert may be in the dry season, and this is often the best season for irrigation.

Regularly flowing rivers and streams that originate within arid lands are known as "endogenous." Most are fed by springs, many in limestone country, as in the Atlas Mountains in Morocco and parts of Oman. Basaltic rocks also support springs, notably at the Jebel Al Arab on the Jordan-Syria border, and also in Oman. Few endogenous rivers reach the sea, draining instead into inland basins, where the water evaporates or is lost in the ground.

Ephemeral rivers

Most desert streambeds are dry, but they occasionally receive large flows of water and sediment. These flash floods provide important water supplies, but can also be highly destructive. Floods are discussed on pages 32–33.

Groundwater

There are large reservoirs of groundwater beneath some deserts, and only a small fraction of this water reaches the surface in springs or subsurface inputs to lakes. Natural springs and shallow wells have immense historical and actual importance to desert oases. Rather more interesting are *qanat* systems, which were first built many hundreds of years ago to tap groundwaters deep beneath alluvial fans and feed them, through hazardously constructed underground channels to oases at lower levels. The access ducts to these systems, which appear as a series of mounds on the ground, litter the surface of the deserts of Iran, western Pakistan, and parts of Arabia and North Africa.

Much larger groundwater reservoirs were discovered about 50 years ago during oil exploration, and technological advances in pumping and piping have contributed to a huge surge in the use of these reservoirs. The first of the discoveries (from a time before oil exploration), in the 19th century in Australia and the western Sahara, lead to a great leap in optimism about desert development, but the story since has been very mixed. Some of the discoveries, such as the Nubian Aquifer in the eastern Sahara, are apparently huge and, even if they are quite heavily exploited, it may be centuries before they are exhausted. The "Great Manmade River" project in Libya leads this water from wells in the south of the country to the coast, where it is used for irrigation, domestic, and industrial supply. But new techniques in dating groundwater have shown us that the water in all these aquifers is thousands of years old (some of it many thousands), so even the Nubian Aquifer is a finite resource, which is not being renewed. Most other desert aquifers are smaller, and many, such as those in Saudi Arabia, are being depleted very quickly and yielding more and more saline water as they delve deeper into the ground. The water in the Great Artesian Basin in Australia has also been found to be very old, dating to sometime in the Quaternary period when rainfall was greater, and it is almost all too salty to be used for irrigation.

▼ *The River Niger,*
western Africa's principal
river and the third
longest river in Africa,
flows through
the western Sahara
Desert for part of its
course. The river is an
essential source of water
to millions of people.

DROUGHT

Drought, understood in a simple way, could be said to be permanent and severe in the very dry deserts. But "drought" understood in that way is not a very useful term; after all people do not expect it to rain in places that are almost always dry. Drought is better understood as a dry period in an area or at a season that is usually wetter. Drought, understood like that, is a feature of semiarid areas, where pastures and agricultural crops depend on rainfall at least in one season. Everyone who works in these areas fears drought, so it is strange that a scientific definition is so difficult. But it is. A drought may be "less rain than expected," but by how much, and over what length of time? Some crops can survive droughts that kill others; some soils store or yield up water to crops more efficiently than others; some parts of the landscape collect water; others shed it. Should a definition of drought be specific to a particular crop, soil or position in the landscape? A definition is important to those who could claim some kind of drought compensation, or to agencies who need to gear up to get help into drought-hit areas.

Predicting droughts

Droughts (whatever scientists decide they are) happen erratically, which makes planning very difficult. There were severe droughts in Australia in 1902, 1912–15, 1965–67 and 1972; the worst drought for two centuries began in 1983. In the early 1990s, northeast Brazil had its worst drought since 1583, and southern Africa had a terrible drought in 1992. In the Sahel region of Africa a "dry spell" lasted through the 1970s and 1980s, but the rainfall fell even further in the early 1970s and in 1984. Every Sahelian farmer can give a 20- or 30-year history of droughts in his village, each with a name like "the killer" attached to it. Names like do not exaggerate: thousands, even hundreds of thousands died as a result of the Sahelian droughts; in Sudan, many villages were abandoned after the 1984 drought and even in the good years after were not re-occupied. Sudanese villagers casually talk about the times before and after that drought, so big was the disruption it

WORST DROUGHTS				
Region	Country	Year	Disaster	Number of fatalities
Shensi, Honan, Kansu	China	1928	Drought	3,000,000
Calcutta, Bengal	India	1942	Drought	1,500,000
Bengal	India	1900	Drought	1,250,000
South Ukraine, Volga	Soviet Union	1921	Drought	1,200,000
North	China	1920	Drought	500,000
–	India	1965	Drought	500,000
–	India	1966	Drought	500,000
–	India	1967	Drought	500,000
Wollo, Tigray, Eritrea, Shoa, Gonder, Harerge, Sidamo	Ethiopia	1984	Drought	300,000
Wollo, Tigray, Kangra	Ethiopia	1974		200,000

caused. There will be more droughts, long and short. Although meteorologists do not know when they will arrive, some clues are emerging: droughts, even in Africa, and with more certainty in Australia are linked to the ENSO (El Niño-Southern Oscillation) rhythm of changes in warm- and cold-water distribution in the equatorial Pacific, and more and more clues are emerging that allow it to be forecast.

Coping with drought

People in the dry lands have had to learn to live with drought by careful management of resources. Most pastoralists have adopted a nomadic habit, searching out where the rain has fallen and moving their stock to those places. If they have bases in agriculture, for instance in better watered valleys or in the semiarid areas where rain-fed agriculture is possible, then they may take part in "transhumance," in which they take their flocks on an annual trek to better pastures that are covered by snow in the winter or may have been too dry in the dry season. Pastoralists of all kinds are notoriously well informed about what is happening, and particularly about the rainfall, in a very large area (because they need to be). The very few hunter-gatherers who remain as such have much the same habit. Rain-fed agriculture is difficult in deserts, with two exceptions. One is runoff-farming, in which runoff from valley sides is collected in valley bottoms to irrigate crops. These people may actually thrive in a drought that denudes their hillslopes, because heavy rains may then run off the slopes without hindrance. Another group of rainfed farmers takes advantage only of the wet years to plant their crops. In central Sudan, these people use light sandy soils, into which rain penetrates, but does not so easily evaporate. They collect a crop as rarely as one year in three or four.

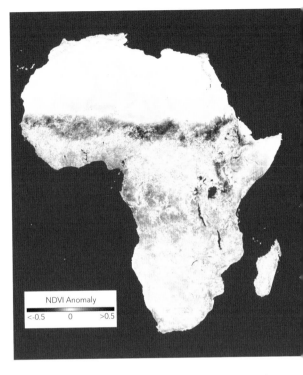

NDVI Anomaly

<-0.5   0   >0.5

▲ *The African drought of 1984–85 shows clearly in this Multi-spectral Drought Index image from August 1984. Dark reddish-brown areas indicate unhealthy vegetation relative to a normal year. The drought withered crops in the Sahel (along the southern border of the Sahara Desert) hit Ethiopia, Sudan, and Somalia especially hard.*

23

DRY LANDSCAPES

Unlike all other landscapes, those in the deserts and the polar regions are laid bare for inspection: hills and valleys, geological structures, and the colors of rock, soil, and sand all become very much more obvious. In the tropical deserts, many soils are red in color: the redness comes from the oxidization of iron. In other deserts, rock and stone surfaces are colored a very dark red or black. This is "desert varnish," a concentration of iron and manganese derived either from the rocks themselves, or from dust deposited on them and fixed there by bacteria and lichens, which only spring to life when they are wetted. Most desert varnish is very old, but some has formed fairly recently. Ancient petroglyphs (carvings or drawings on rock) in Australia and the southwestern United States have been found shrouded in desert varnish.

DESERT LANDFORMS

Many desert landscapes are boringly featureless, or very gently undulating, but others are filled with extraordinary rock formations, sculpted by tectonic upheavals or by surface processes. The most distinctive agent of these in deserts is the wind. Only on coasts does the wind have the same latitude to create landscapes. In the driest of deserts wind moves more material than water. All the dustiest places on Earth are in the extreme deserts. About a third of the desert is covered with sand dunes, and the wind has elsewhere left its mark on solid, hard rocks. When rain does come, floods may sweep down desert valleys, collecting up debris, which they then spread out over the plains. The rivers take the finest bits of debris and the salts to dry lakes.

Unique landscapes

Some desert landscapes are very familiar: the deep, multi-colored gash of the Grand Canyon in the southwestern United States; the vast red mass of Uluru (Ayers Rock) in central Australia; the fluted towers of the Ahaggar in southern Algeria; the curvaceous, repetitious russet sand seas of the Namib, Sahara, or Arabia. Those who know the desert acknowledge the unique beauty of these places, but they also know many other incredibly beautiful desert places, many with unique landforms.

▶ *Rock is weathered (broken down) in three main ways: (A) biological; (B) chemical and (C) physical, which in deserts means by heating and cooling, wetting, and drying; and prising apart by salts which crystallize as water evaporates. Biological action (which is weak in deserts) creates a soil. Chemical action (B), which is also weak in deserts because of the near-absence of water, dissolves the more soluble parts of the rock, which are then removed in groundwater. Physical weathering (C) is the most potent force in deserts, prising pieces of rock apart.*

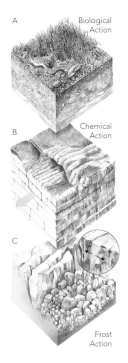

A — Biological Action

B — Chemical Action

C — Frost Action

Desert landforms are of two main types: those in which water is the main agent of erosion; and those in which it is wind. Wind and water, nonetheless, have collaborated over many thousands of years to produce the elements of the modern landscape. There are some desert landscapes in which wind dominates as the agent of erosion. There are others where water wins out. There are yet others in which they are in almost equal partnership. But there is more to collaboration than that: material eroded and moved by one medium, may, thousands of years later, be moved by the other.

It is now clear to geomorphologists that most of the sands and dusts that are moved by the wind today were derived, at some distant time, by water erosion. Sands and silts were taken from mountains by water, deposited on great spreads of sediment in the plains, and then blown into dunes, or blown away as dust. A more recent geological phenomenon has been the attack by the wind on water-laid, still-soft deposits in Quaternary lakes. These deposits provided dust, but also soft rocks, which when abraded by the wind, form into wind-eroded forms, known as "yardangs."

"Hammadas" are desert plateaus whose surfaces have been attacked only lightly by water erosion, but on which there are "desert pavements." These are thin coverings of stones overlying much finer soils, and are believed to have been formed by a combination of water-wash and wind erosion of the fine material (concentrating the stones at the surface), by the upward movement of stones through the soil as it was heated and cooled, or wetted and dried, and the settling and washing down of dust that fell on the surface, which slowly lifted the stones.

Weathering

Another landform-creating process that is laid bare to see in deserts is "weathering." This is the term adopted by geomorphologists to describe the breakdown of rocks and sediments by a number of processes. Rock is broken down in various ways. One is the daily extremes of heat and cold, which can crack rocks and pebbles. It has been claimed that the north-south orientation of cracks in Arizona desert rocks proves the effectiveness of this process. In some high-altitude deserts, such as the Karakoram of Pakistan, frost shattering of rock can occur. Similarly, rock disintegration can occur as salt crystals grow in the cracks between rocks and prize them open. These weathering processes can produce bizarre landforms, like mushroom rocks, which form when salty water seeps only into the lower part of an upstanding rock. The lower part is then split apart by salt crystallization, leaving the upper part intact.

◀ *The Colorado River* *is primarily responsible for the breathtaking Grand Canyon. Fed by mountain waters, the river has carved down into the desert surface through rock strata that represent hundreds of millions of years.*

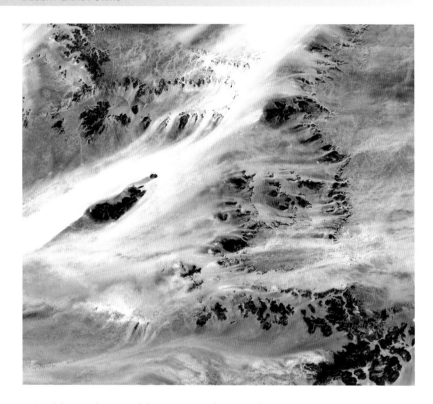

Dry lakes in deserts exhibit a variety of strange features. Some of these lakes are almost salt-free, and these are so level that they have been used as racetracks. On a small number of these there are "wandering rocks," great angular blocks weighing up to 700 lbs (320 kg), which move over the surface leaving tracks behind them. The best-known site is Racetrack Playa in the Mojave Desert in the southwestern United States. No one has seen them move, but it is now thought that they move on the very rare occasions when high winds coincide with a thin layer of water on the smooth surface.

On salty, dry lakes, a thick salt-crust develops; as the salts crystallize they expand upward, downward, and outward, and the lateral pressure of the crystallization then produces polygons of various sizes. The polygons are any-where between a few inches and several miles across. The salt crust eventually prevents further evaporation of water, and as a result the surface crust may conceal boggy ground beneath. These salt lakes are known as "sabkha" in the Arabian Peninsula.

▲ **Dominating** the north of Africa is the largest area of dry land on Earth: the Sahara Desert. Stretching across the Sahara are vast plains of sand and gravel, seas of sand dunes, and barren rocky mountains. The satellite images shows a typical desert landscape in the hyperarid desert of northern Chad. There are rocky, jagged outcrops (dark); weathered soil (red); and a wide stream of sand (light colors) sweeping in from the northeast.

Even if they flow only very occasionally, desert rivers have tremendous power to erode and carry sediment. This power has created deep gorges and delivered large amounts of coarse sediment to alluvial fans, deposited where the mountains end and open out into large, flat plains. Four factors ensure the impact of these rivers: the intensity of much of desert rainfall; the barrenness of most desert slopes; the amount of debris that accumulates between rainstorms; and the "armoring" of desert streambeds by smooth pavements of pebbles, resulting in very fast transfer of water and sediment.

But, like many features of deserts, much of the river erosion we see today was probably accomplished, not so much by rivers in the present arid landscape, as by rivers in wetter periods in the past. Huge meander scars in many deserts, within which the modern river is a tiny trickle, and great river networks that barely function, as in Niger, are some of the evidence that shows that rivers were much fuller in the past. On the north shore of Lake Mega-Chad, a huge delta, the Angamma, is stranded above a vast dry lake, in what is now almost lifeless desert. Hippopotamus and crocodile bones can be dug out of the now-hardened mud round the edge of the delta from valley sides devoid of plants.

Badlands

Some of the most distinctive desert landscapes are the badlands—barren "moonscapes," devoid of vegetation and dissected by dense networks of rills and deep steep-sided gullies. These landscapes are found throughout western North America—particularly on the Great Plains and Colorado Plateau—as well as in Mexico, China, and Spain, although they cover less than five percent of desert areas. The well-known sites, such as the Badlands National Park in South Dakota, have been formed in soft, saline shale rock, on which plants find it difficult to grow. Some badlands are formed where intense cultivation or grazing has laid bare the soil.

Erosion rates in badlands are extraordinarily high; 0.08 to 0.8 inches (2 to 20 millimetres) depth of soil may be removed each year, despite the fact that rainwater runoff is rare. The rate of erosion may be so rapid that formation of new soil is impossible. The arid climate further hinders the growth of vegetation. Erosion occurs both on the surface as "sheetwash" and beneath it as "piping" or "tunnel" erosion. Tunnel erosion occurs when rainwater seeps into deep cracks in the soil. The cracks are enlarged and elongated into tunnels, some of which are more like caves—as much as 100 feet (30 metres) long and 6.5 feet (2 metres) wide and high.

Other river-formed landscapes in deserts may be less spectacular, but are nonetheless distinctive. In the mountains, most slopes down to the dry streams are straight and divided by sharp crests. More distinctive and much more puzzling, but so inconspicuous they are barely recognizable from the ground are "pediments"—gently sloping surfaces cut across hard rock on the flanks of large basins. Hard to identify from the ground, they are much more recognizable from the air, and their formation is still mysterious.

Deposition by water

Short-lived, fast-flowing streams acquire a heavy load of sediment as they rush down from highlands. When they leave the confines of hills and reach flat, wide, desert plains, they spread out and lose their power to carry sediment. Large amounts of cobbles, sand, silt, and clay are then deposited across the plain. These are "alluvial fans"—cones of coarse sediment that have been dumped on the plains by overloaded streams.

▼ *An excellent aerial view of an alluvial fan, taken over Gansu Province, China. The fan shape is built up the river, which deposits sediment when it spreads out over the plain. The sediment often blocks the stream, diverting the water sometimes to the left, and sometimes to the right, and these diversions, over many years, create the fan.*

Although they occur in many other environments, alluvial fans are more visible in deserts, and usually much bigger. They can be single, or joined to others in large fan complexes. Single fans can be many miles across at their base, and rise many hundreds of feet above the plain. The streams that form them take different courses each time they flow, as sediment blocks one or another earlier channel. This distributes the sediment sometimes here, sometimes there, across the fan. Sometimes the stream carries so much sediment it is better called a mudflow, and these can carry huge boulders, the size of large houses, well out onto the fan.

Fan-shaped landscapes

On many fans, if not most, the parent stream has cut down (incised itself) below the level of the fan. In many places it has done this repeatedly, so that newer fans are incised into older ones. Pebbles or boulders on the older fan surfaces, stranded higher and higher above the incised stream, accumulate darker and darker coverings of desert varnish, so that fans of different age and isolation create a rich pattern of dark and light surfaces. The causes of incision are many: uplift of the mountain, changes in flow, or changes in the amount of debris.

Alluvial fans can take a long time to form and their deposits are therefore an important record of environmental history. For instance, the Milner Creek fan in the White Mountains of California is still growing after 700,000 years. Alluvial fans are important for groundwater resources, a property recognized many thousands of years ago in southwest Asia by *qanat* diggers. These amazing people would recognize that there was water within the fan, dig a well down to it, and then conduct the water through a gently sloping tunnel (the *qanat* or *falaj*, see pages 9 and 20–21) down to an oasis.

FLOODS

In the desert rain may be scarce, but it can come in a deluge. It has been said that in deserts more people have drowned in rivers than have died of thirst.

The reasons for the intensity of desert rains are various, but a common one is that rapidly rising hot desert air, cooling and condensing as it rises, causes highly localized rainfall, if moisture has been brought in from the oceans. Rainstorms are often just a few miles across, and fall on ground with little plant cover to absorb the downfall. When the intensity of the rain exceeds the rate at which the soil can absorb the water, there is runoff. This is rapidly taken across the bare soil to small watercourses, which all reach the main courses within a short time of each other and so concentrate the flood downstream. In the deserts of North Africa and southwest Asia, cold fronts can bring rain that lasts for days.

▼ *Temporary floodwater* sits in a depression in the Namib Desert. Deserts are prone to flash flooding, partly because the lack of vegetation ensures that water runs off sloping ground very quickly.

Flash floods

In the Mojave Desert in January 2005 a huge flash flood swept away houses, bridges and motorways. Levees and other flood-control structures were also swept away. President Bush had to declare a disaster of federal proportions. It caused damage worth $80 million.

There are many other examples of severe desert flooding. In the same month, huge floods inundated several valleys around Al Madina (Medina) in Saudi Arabia during the final days of the annual *Hajj* pilgrimage. In 1990, it was reported that tens of thousands of people had been evacuated in southern Somalia when their villages, which had been built in a normally arid area, were submerged under the floodwaters of the Juba River. A flood in northern Sinai in 1973 swept away a bridge on the railway the Turks had built six decades before, and killed some Bedouin camped in the dry riverbed. A very large flood in Tunisia in 1969 cut the country in two. All the main roads to the south were swept away. Some 600 were said to have been killed 70,000 homes were destroyed and 300,000 people were made refugees. Studies of "palaeofloods" in the desert show that there have been truly horrific floods in places like central Australia, in the not-so-distant past. A gorge on the Fitzroy River in Western Australia contains deposits that show that there must have been six floods of between 100 cubic feet (3 cubic metres) per second during the last 2,000 years, which are some of the biggest floods ever recorded for basins of that size.

Flash floods carry great loads of sediment. The reason is that soil accumulates on the surface between the rare floods and is then suddenly washed away all at once. In 1973, for example, on the Wadi Medjerdah in Tunisia, a storm—something that occurs there on average only once every 200 years—produced a deposit of silt over an area of about 53 square miles (140 square kilometres). Flash floods frequently deposit 3-foot- (1-metre-) high mounds of gravel on desert roads, incurring large costs in clearing them.

Three facts show just how important wind is to desert landscapes. First, they produce much more dust than any other environment. All the dustiest places are in deserts. Second, about a quarter of the world's deserts are buried by wind-blown sand. Hundreds of square miles of dunes, most over 10 feet (3 metres) in height, each progressing at 50 feet (15 metres) every year, is not an unusual occurrence. Third, there are smaller, but still large areas of wind-eroded rock, in Iran and the central Sahara, and very many much smaller areas in places like Patagonia, northern Canada, and China.

Wind is more effective in deserts than in other regions, not because it is any stronger than in wetter environments (although it can be very strong when it flows through mountain passes), but because dry surfaces and a lack of protective vegetation make it more effective. In the very dry

▲ **Pillars like these** are formed by wind erosion. In this case the wind has created a pillar out of an ancient dune deposit, which has been cemented together by calcium carbonate (from shells). A modern, still active, dune can be seen on the right. It will soon move over and bury the pillar. The site is in the south of the Wahiba Sand Sea in Oman.

deserts wind moves much more sediment than water. In the wetter desert margins, water takes over as the main agent of erosion. As deserts get wetter, so does the power of water, and water wins out in semiarid areas.

Wind, sand and dust near the ground

The wind picks up dry sand and dust where it finds it, when it blows faster than a threshold of about 20 feet (6 metres) per second. This figure is for sands with common diameters and for wind velocity measured at 6 feet (2 metres) above the ground. The term "sand" is applied to rock fragments between 0.008 and 0.08 inches (0.2–2 millimeters) in diameter. Grains of dust are smaller. In special circumstances, like Racetrack Playa, mentioned on page 28, the wind can move boulders. Even in more normal circumstances, as on some parts of the Peruvian coast and in Antarctica, high winds move small pebbles. But most winds are not so strong, and most cannot move anything bigger than sand.

The first grains to be lifted by the wind from a mixture of sand and dust on the surface are of the sands. The small grains of dust cohere more firmly than do sand grains, and so are not the first to leave a mixture. The sand grains can be lifted by two processes that are stronger than the forces that hold them together. One is the difference in air pressure caused when the wind blows over a grain. The second is the "shear" of the wind across the surface. When the first sand grains rise into the wind, they acquire some of its energy and bring it back when they fall back to the surface. This energy lifts more grains in an accelerating process until the near-ground air is thick with sand grains bouncing off each other and the surface. The thickest "cloud" of moving sand is only a few centimetres deep, so that you can eat your sandwiches in a sand storm (although not a dust storm) without getting sand in them, while your ankles are being sandblasted. The whole process is called "saltation" from the Latin *saltare* (to leap).

In most situations it is the leaping sand that liberates the dust. Most dust-sized particles are held in tough clods held together by chemical and physical forces between the grains, or in surface crusts held together by algae and lichens. The clods and crusts are either too large or too heavy to be lifted, or tough enough to resist the wind, unless it carries bombarding sand. The energy in the saltating sand grains, brought down from higher windspeeds above the surface, break apart clods or crusts and release the dust. Once set free by sandblasting, the dust travels high into the air, and if it is fine enough it may travel many times round the Earth. It is dust that gives us all our red sunsets.

DUST

Dust is lifted into the air in three common ways. The great stream of dust that comes out of northern Chad is lifted by a "low-level jet," an air stream that is no more than 3,300 feet (1,000 meters) deep, funnelled between two mountains. There are three more common ways in which dust is raised. The first is the "dust devil," a small whirl of dust, termed *"djinns"* in Arabic, or "willy-willies" in Australia. These are small scale on Earth (no more than a few feet across (although sometimes wider), but they are more common and effective on Mars. Dust devils are like small tornadoes, but never reach anything like their ferocity. They have a small calm "eye," surrounded by a ring of sinking air, and farther out another of rising air. The velocity in the rings can reach 73 feet (22 meters) per second—capable of lifting small pebbles.

The second common way in which dust is raised is by thunderstorms, and it is these that give rise to the frightening walls of dust that sweep across places like the Sahel and Arizona. They are now known internationally by the colloquial Sudanese name *"haboob."* In Arizona and the Sahel *haboobs* are brought on by the first storms of the summer rainy season, before the rain has brought on the crops or the grass cover. A current of turbulent air precedes the thunderstorm and raises the dust.

The third common way in which dust is raised is common in northern deserts like those in China, North Africa, southwestern Asia, and southern Australia. This is the cold front, which can also raise great walls of dust, sweeping across the country at speeds of 40–50 miles (70–80 kilometers) per hour, suddenly turning day to night when they arrive, and creating enormous havoc.

Dust sources and sinks

In the last few years it has been discovered conclusively that most "soil-derived" dust comes from the deserts. The term "soil-derived" is used to distinguish it from other sorts of dust that come from grass and forest fires and industrial pollution. It is now thought that less than 10 percent of soil-derived dust comes from disturbance as from plowing or wind erosion of agricultural soils. The biggest source, by far, is the dry bed of Lake Mega-Chad, the remains of a huge Holocene lake. The situation there is almost unique: the low-level jet (very strong wind), whistling down from the north between the Tibesti and Ennedi mountains, passes over very light, friable deposits of diatomite, laid down in the ancient freshwater lake. There are other intensely active sources of dust in the deserts, almost all old lakebeds, but none is nearly as intense a source. They occur in the western Sahara, southeastern Arabia, and the

▲ **Satellite image** of a dust storm over the Indian-Pakistan border. During such storms, dust can be transported thousands of miles.

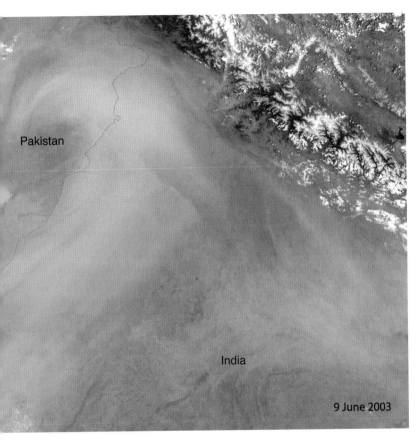

Pakistan

India

9 June 2003

Gobi Desert. There are smaller sources in Patagonia, northern Namibia, and Lake Eyre in Australia.

These sources spew out dust in great plumes downwind. The dust from Mega-Chad passes first over the Sahel, in a wind known there as the *Harmattan*, which is at its worst between March and May each year. It may bring meningitis to Sahelian villagers, but it also brings them enough potassium and calcium for their sparse crops. The *Harmattan* dust then acts as the main source of nutrients to the Ghanaian rainforests. What remains travels across the Atlantic to fertilize the forests of the northeastern Amazon basin. Another stream passes from farther west in West Africa, taking enough dust to give Barbados a bad reputation for asthma, and on to Florida, where it makes up a handsome proportion of Florida's pollution.

Dust from the northern Sahara travels to Sicily (where you can see it on cars every summer), and on to Crete and the Levant. Some of this dust is even swept, on a few days every year, to northern Europe, where it sometimes brings "blood rain" or pink snow.

Dust from western China travels out over the Loess Plateau (laid down by much bigger dust storms in the Quaternary), over Beijing, where it mixes with pollution to give an unpleasant haze, and then out over Korea and to Japan, where it is known as "yellow sand." Some of it reaches Hawaii, whose forests, like those of Ghana, are fertilized by it, and may eventually, in some years, reach the western United States. Dust from Australia travels to New Zealand, where it sometimes discolors the snow in the Southern Alps, and to Antarctica.

▼ *A dust storm* sweeps across a large area of Oklahoma and Texas. Airborne dust particles are very small, but en masse they are dangerous. Sweeping in from the desert, these rolling clouds of dust can paralyze transport systems, create medical emergencies, and leave residents with weeks of cleaning-up and repairing damage.

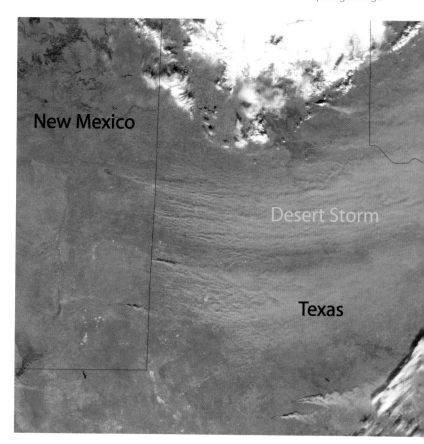

New Mexico

Desert Storm

Texas

▶ *A sand storm arrives behind a shepherd and his goats near the village of Kamaka, Mali. It begins with a huge wave of sand and is followed by a violent rainstorm.*

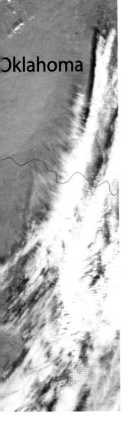

Oklahoma

Manmade dust

Surfaces disturbed by people can barely compete with these immense clouds of natural dust. World War II battles in North Africa, and the first Gulf War in Saudi Arabia and Kuwait are known, nonetheless, to have kicked up large clouds of dust. Off-road vehicles in the Mojave Desert do sometimes cause small duststorms that extend for over 20 miles (30 kilometers) and cover 115 square miles (300 square kilometers). The worst two examples of people-generated dust clouds are the Aral Sea, desiccated by the withdrawal of water upstream in Central Asia, and Lake Owens in the northern Mojave of California, which was drained to supply Los Angeles with water, and which almost completely dried up by 1926. The lake now produces 900,000 to 8 million tons of dust a year, detectable as a plume 25 miles (40 kilometers) downwind.

During the last ice age when winds were generally stronger, the deserts were bigger and glacial meltwater streams produced great bare expanses of silty alluvium, much more dust moved round the world. Great depths of loess accumulated in places like northern China, northern Europe and Russia, the western Great Plains of the United States, New Zealand, and Argentina. In China, thick loess, with an average depth of 260–300 feet (80–100 meters), covers more than 105,000 square miles (273,000 square kilometers) on the Shensi Plateau.

DUNES

Sand dunes can be anything from 3 feet (1 meter) high and about 6.5 x 6.5 feet (2 x 2 meters) in plan to 1,300 feet (400 meters) high and tens of miles long. The simplest of them are accumulations in the lee of bushes (known as *nabkha* in colloquial Arabic), large rocks or hills, such as the Draa Malichig dune in Mauritania, which is 60 miles (100 kilometers) long. Others start as accumulations of sand in shallow surface depressions, or when a sudden, small, but strong burst of wind sweeps sand into small piles. Once a mound of sand has formed, it attracts more sand, and will then replicate itself downwind as a result of the way that it disturbs the airflow. Thus, sand dunes often occur in assemblages of regular pattern and similar height.

Sand and wind

Dunes of different types occur because of differences in annual wind pattern and sand supply. Where the wind blows in one direction throughout the year and sand is plentiful, sinuous ridges are formed at right angles to the wind ("transverse dunes".) If the sand is scarce, and the wind still very constant, the ridges break down into isolated crescent—or horseshoe-shaped dunes known as "barchans." These are a relatively rare type of dune, but are well known

▼ **Dunes** in the Great Eastern Sand Sea (erg) in the northwestern Sahara. These dunes have been built up by winds from the northeast in winter and variable winds in summer. The tallest dunes are probably several thousand years old.

because of their speed of movement. Sand eroded from the gentle windward slope of the barchan dune is deposited on the steep lee face and the dune "rolls" downwind. The speed of movement is governed by the size of the dune and the speed of the wind. Small barchans less than about 3 feet (1 meter) high may move 150 feet (50 meters) per year, although a more common figure for an average 30-foot- (10-meter-) high barchan is 15–30 feet (5–10 meters) per year. Barchan dunes do not grow in height indefinitely but tend to reach an equilibrium size, which depends on environmental conditions, such as wind strength.

Where winds come from two principal directions during the year, say from the northwest in summer and the southwest in winter, as they do in northern Sinai in Egypt, the dune is blown first in the one direction and then the other, and extends in a direction which more or less bisects the two wind directions, which in northern Sinai is toward the east-north-east. These are known as "longitudinal dunes," a name given to them because they were first recognized in the Western Desert of Egypt, where they are aligned north to south.

Where the wind direction comes from many directions in a yearly cycle, the dune pattern is much more confused. In low dunes, a pattern of overlapping ridges develops, each at right angles to one of the winds, the height of each set being in rough proportion to the strength of the wind that forms them and to the length of time it blows. When there is more sand, massive star dunes accumulate. These dunes are pyramidal in form, with long, sinuous arms radiating from the summit. They become sand traps, accumulating mass and losing little sand to the surrounding desert plains. They cover large parts of the Great Eastern Sand Sea in Algeria, where they occasionally reach as much as 3,300 feet (1,000 meters) wide and 1,000 feet (300 meters) high.

Seas of sand

Most dunes are gathered together in vast areas termed "sand seas," or *ergs* in North-African Arabic. The largest sand seas are in North Africa, Arabia, and the desert basins of Central Asia. There are also examples in Australia and Namibia. The greatest number of sand seas occurs in the Sahara, but the largest single sand sea is the Rub' Al Khālī (Empty Quarter) in Arabia, which covers an area of 215,000 square miles (560,000 square kilometers). There are many smaller bodies of dunes, best termed dune fields. Examples are the Kelso and Algodones dune fields in the Mojave Desert, and the Great Sand Dunes in Colorado.

Most sand seas occur in large depressions in the desert, to which much of the sand has been brought by rivers, although some sand may also have been swept in by winds across nearby plateaus. These "streams" of sand cross the Sahara, the Mojave, the Australian and the Namib deserts, taking sand from one sand sea to another. The Saharan sand flows cross many thousands of miles, and leaves the Sahara for the Atlantic Ocean off Mauritania. The Namib Sand Sea is fed by a flow northward from the Orange River. Sand seas accumulate over thousands of years. The deposits of the Great Eastern Sand Sea in Algeria probably took more than 10,000 years to accumulate and, if spread out evenly, would be 140 feet (43 meters) thick. In most sand seas, generations of dunes are imposed one on another, the older ones being remnants of wind regimes in the distant past.

In most sand seas, only about 60 percent of the area is actually covered with dunes. The areas between the dunes may be sand sheets (undulating plains of sand) or stony desert pavements. The dunes in most sand seas are a mixture of all the main types. There is also a great mixture of sizes of dune, all the way from dunes 3 feet (1 meter) high up to dunes over 2,500 feet (800 meters) high.

▼ *A massive dune* *towers above the Sossus Vlei in the Namib Desert of southern Africa. The few thorn trees will do little to halt the slow progress of this huge dune. It is probably moving at less than 3 ft (1 m) each year.*

Dunes as problems

Migrating dunes can present a major threat to any fields, forests, highways, railroads, or pipelines that happen to get in their way. The most serious problems occur around towns and villages where the surface is disturbed, loosening the sand, and removing any cover of plants that might be there. Funneling of the sand along streets and high turbulence around buildings may abrade building materials and make living conditions very uncomfortable. In the sheltered zones in the lee of buildings, sand may accumulate and block roads. Dust is also swept into desert towns and trapped between the buildings. The wind that enters a city is often more dusty than the one that leaves it. Communication lines are particularly vulnerable to dune encroachment—the blocking of roads often requires detours or costly removal measures.

Stabilizing dunes

The effort put into stabilizing dunes has intensified in the Middle East during the past 30 or 40 years as a result of economic growth and increasing development in the sandy areas. As well as the physical removal of dunes by bulldozer and dump truck, many other alternatives have been tested. Sand fences constructed upwind of areas requiring protection have proven successful in some places, but the fences are eventually buried by the sand they trap, so further fences must be built on top of the original ones. Fences must be carefully managed to prevent the creation of very large dunes in this way, which may then begin to move and threaten installations. Another form of control is to spray the sand with oil or specially designed chemicals, but these surfaces also soon get buried by new sand, and the spraying is very expensive. The most effective and permanent method of stabilization is to plant vegetation, but when water is scarce (as it usually is in the desert), the plants are costly to maintain.

WIND EROSION

The power of the wind to erode, or alter the landscape, has long been underestimated. The wind erodes not so much because of its own power, but because of abrasion by the sediment that it carries. In deserts the abundance of loose material makes wind erosion a very powerful force. This power manifests itself in a wide variety of wind-sculpted landforms, from streamlined hills to sandblasted stones, as well as the excavation of hollows.

The high-velocity impact of saltating sand grains, in the small zone near the surface where they are concentrated, is a very efficient form of erosion. On soft materials, like mud bricks, abrasion can be evident in very few years, or even months. Stones and rocks on the desert surface are grooved and polished by sandblasting, and are shaped into ventifacts (wind-faceted stones). If soft (like mud bricks), abrasion can be evident in a few years, or even less. The eroded rocks can be identified by their smooth faces (on uniformly hard material) or fretting (on material that has variable hardness). Smooth faces intersect at sharp angles. The limited height of the "saltation curtain" means that this process of erosion is most efficient below 8–12 inches (20–30 centimeters). Evidence for this comes from the undercutting of rock at this height.

▼ *Large sand grains* blown by desert winds bounce only 3 ft (1 m) high and erode the thin neck that is characteristic of the zeugen or pedestal. Fine sand blows higher but erodes less.

Yardangs

On a larger scale, the wind erodes small hillocks known as yardangs. These are hills that have been abraded by the wind into streamlined, tapered forms. They occur where the wind comes generally from one direction throughout the year. Vast fields of yardangs aligned parallel to the wind can be found on the Peruvian coast, in Iran, and in Western Desert of Egypt. Yardangs range in size from as small as 3 feet (1 meter) in length, to up to several miles. The best examples of "mega-yardangs" are found around the Tibesti Mountains in the central Sahara, where parallel arrays of yardangs, spaced about 3,300

feet (1,000 meters) apart, cover a total area of 260,000 square miles (650,000 square kilometers). These forms can reach 660 feet (200 meters) in height, and many miles long. Most yardangs are carved from soft, loose rocks, but the Tibesti yardangs are cut in hard, ancient sandstones. Yardangs occur most commonly in corridors of sand movement where high winds hurl the sediment against the rock faces. The Tibesti yardangs are therefore likely to be hundreds of the thousands of years old.

Powerful localized wind erosion can take place when a surface has been weakened by a break in the crust or by the removal of vegetation. In the Kalahari Desert and Great Plains of the United States, scouring by the wind—or "deflation"—has created large semicircular, elongated hollows, or "pans" up to 3,300 feet (1,000 meters) in diameter, which are devoid of vegetation. In the arid Sahara, where there is no vegetation to temper deflation, and where there was no vegetation for many thousands of years in the Quaternary, very large basins are thought to have been excavated by the wind, an example being the Qattara Depression in northern Egypt.

Wind erosion is a practical problem on the desert margins, where fields are laid bare after sowing (at least in some years). In these areas, sandy soils are very common (developed on the ancient dunes from the Quaternary), and they are both the easiest soils to work with a hoe (which is all that most farmers have), and those that absorb and make available most water for crops. But they are also the most vulnerable to being eroded by the wind. In Sudan, many field boundaries, which have not been eroded because they are protected by bushes, may stand 3–6.5 feet (1–2 meters) above the eroded fields between. While wind erosion is clearly happening very quickly, it is difficult to decide whether the lost soil equates to lost crop production. Wind erosion also occurs on other semiarid soils, as in the western Great Plains of the USA, where it reached a horrifying climax during the Dust Bowl of the 1930s. The chief problem there, however, was the dust that was the product of the wind erosion, which caused health and esthetic problems in nearby towns. Semiarid parts of China suffer the same problems.

SOILS

Desert soils have four distinguishing characteristics. First, large quantities of dust are continually falling on them. This dust usually contains different constituents from the rock debris with which it mingles. Second, because they are less moist, desert soils are less chemically altered than humid soils. Third, not being leached continuously with water, they are generally saltier than humid soils (sometimes very much more so). Finally, because chemical alteration, leaching, and erosion take place slowly, desert soils have retained many more features from the past than soils where the evidence is washed away.

The uppermost layers of most uncultivated desert soils, away from the main valleys, are quite rich in soluble salts. In humid soils, these salts are washed out entirely. The near-surface soil in very dry desert soils, like those in the Egyptian Sahara, has concentrations of common salt (sodium chloride), a very soluble salt, as cooks know. In slightly wetter areas, such as southern Tunisia and parts of New Mexico, the common salt has been washed out of the upper soil and gypsum (hydrated calcium sulphate) occurs at the surface, or in a layer just beneath, to where it has been washed down. On the wetter edges of the desert, as in most of the Mediterranean, large swathes of Australia, and in much of the southwestern United States, the characteristic horizon is formed by calcretes (calcium carbonate), because common salt and gypsum have been leached away.

Some desert soils have other hard subsurface horizons, which date from a wetter past. These horizons include laterites (rich in iron) and silcretes (rich in silica). In Australia, silcrete horizons contain gem-quality opal. Like calcretes, laterites and silcretes are as hard as rock.

River valley soils

In the alluvium along the main river valleys, there are two main types of soil. In some hollows in semiarid lands—where there is not too much salt—silica washed down in drainage water combines to form clays that hold organic matter tightly together. These black clay soils are "vertisols." They also form through the breakdown of basalt rock in semiarid conditions. They are very fertile when irrigated and support cotton growing in the Deccan Plateau of India and in the central Sudan.

Other types of soil in the alluvium are less fertile. Most alluvium is cultivable and can yield good crops when irrigated, but where the water table is close to the surface, salts are brought to the surface in evaporating water, where they accumulate. This happens in natural hollows in the

▼ *Cones rise* from the stem of a tumboa plant (Welwitschia mirabilis) on the pebbly surface of part of the Namib Desert. Many desert soils have this kind of surface, created partly when the wind removes the fine grains, partly when occasional storms wash grains away, and partly when pebbles rise to the surface as the soil is intensely heated and cooled.

landscape, but it is now associated more with over-irrigation or inadequate drainage. Many thousands of acres of land have been made totally unproductive by the accumulation of a white cover of salts, some of them dating from the first irrigation schemes in history in Mesopotamia, some much more recent, as around the Aral Sea in Central Asia. There are further problems when the water that has passed through irrigated soils returns to the rivers carrying salt with it. The river water itself becomes saltier, and this creates problems for farmers and wildlife downstream. It is a worldwide problem, as along the Tarim River in western China. The best-known case is the Colorado River in the USA, about which there is an agreement between Mexico and the USA. The USA is contracted to pass water of a low salinity to Mexico, a program that may cost it many billions of dollars.

LIFE IN THE DESERT

Despite their apparent lifelessness, deserts have an amazing variety of well-adapted species. Millions of years of evolution have produced some extraordinary ways of coping with extreme aridity and temperature. These range from the immensely swollen stems of cacti, adapted to store and conserve water, to the specially adapted water-conserving kidneys of some mammals. Deserts are home to anything from tiny insects to large mammals, including representatives of most major groups—even amphibians. Yet the very specialization of such flora and fauna makes them vulnerable to changes in their environments.

PLANTS AND WATER

Plant survival

Life in a desert environment involves many problems for plants. Intense light can damage pigments and high temperatures can disrupt the biochemistry of cells, but the most serious problem of all is desiccation. Water is usually in short supply and adaptations that assist in water conservation are universal among desert plants.

The main problem for plants is that photosynthesis (the production of fundamental sugars using light energy) requires carbon dioxide (CO_2). To ensure efficient uptake of CO_2, the leaves of plants have tiny pores (stomata). But these also allow the evaporation and diffusion of water vapor, a process that occurs rapidly in deserts.

Conserving water

Natural selection in the desert favors plant forms that have reduced the areas of the surfaces through which water may be lost. Some cacti have adopted an extreme form. They have neither leaves nor stems and are almost spherical, providing the least possible surface area for a given volume. The number of stomatal pores is also reduced. One effect of this is to reduce CO_2 intake, so growth rates in these plants are very slow. Other species of plants avoid excessive exposure to the sun and drying winds by growing largely underground.

In general, desert plants have a lower density of stomata in their leaves than plants from other habitats. This helps them to conserve water. But one desert plant, *Welwitschia mirabilis* (Tree Tumbo) from the deserts of Namibia, has a very high density of pores. The bulk of the water supply in this region comes in the form of mist and dew. The high pore density of *Welwitschia* allows it to collect this valuable moisture.

The problem of balancing CO_2 uptake with water loss has been partially overcome by succulents that open their pores only at night, when temperatures are lower, and so lose less water through evaporation. However, the light needed for photosynthesis is not available at night. Instead, the CO_2 absorbed is stored in a temporary form as an organic acid and used during the day. This is called Crassulacean Acid Metabolism (CAM) after the succulent family Crassulaceae in which the process was first described.

Many desert grasses have developed an efficient technique for absorbing CO_2. Like CAM plants, they also fix carbon dioxide into an organic acid, but they then move it to specialized cells deep in their leaves, where it is stored and then used when it is needed for photosynthesis. This method ensures that, for a given amount of growth, these plants need open their stomata only briefly.

Cactus

Cacti have their stomata sunk down into pits (1), which helps cut down transpiration —the evaporation of water— because the air in the pit is protected from air movements above the surface of the leaf and becomes humid. Cacti have tough outer skins, which are often waxy, to cut down water loss. Inside, they are fleshy and capable of storing a lot of moisture. Cacti flower rarely and briefly, after the often violent desert rains. The spherical shape of many cacti maximizes their volume while minimizing their surface area, so that they are ideal water barrels. The ridged body structure of a cactus also plays a role. It may help to reduce tissue damage during the inevitable shrinkage that accompanies water loss.

Cactus spines are actually greatly reduced leaves. Along with the plant's hairs, they hinder air flow and help reflect heat. They also increase the heat-losing surface area of the plant without increasing its water-losing area. In addition, they discourage grazing animals from eating its succulent flesh.

The roots of some xerophytes (plants that are adapted to live in dry conditions) penetrate to a depth of 20 ft (6 m) in their search for water. Other xerophytes have root systems of swollen, water-retaining tubers. Most cacti, however, have a wide-ranging system of fine roots, which are equipped with microscopic hairs (2). The roots may only penetrate a short way underground, but often cover a huge area (3) so that the cactus can quickly replenish its water supplies when water is available. Many cacti, such as the *Echinocereus pulchellus* (4), hide underground in the dry season. Only when conditions are favorable do they extend their green tops above the surface (5). In this way, they combine drought resistance with effective drought evasion.

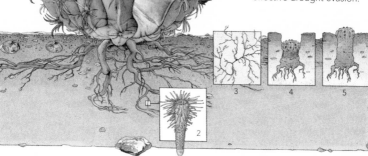

The root systems of desert plants are often extremely deep, tapping supplies of water many feet beneath the surface to replenish their own lost water. Among such plants are the melons and squashes (family Cucurbitaceae). *Prosopis cineraria*, a desert tree in Oman and India, is said to have roots down to 33 feet (10 meters) below the surface. But a surprising number of desert plants do not have deep root systems. The cacti, such as *Opuntia* (Prickly Pear), a native of dry parts of North America (but now widespread in deserts), have shallow, fibrous roots that are largely confined to the upper few inches of soil. These allow the cacti to catch water from dew or brief showers.

▼ *The ocotillo* (Fonquieria splendens), also known as coachwhip and vine cactus, is found in the Sonoran and Chihuahuan deserts. It is well adapted to its desert environment, having a shallow but widespread root system. It is able to shed its leaves quickly during dry spells but can grow them equally quickly when wetter weather arrives.

Perhaps the most remarkable adaptation for a desert plant is the complete absence of roots found in *Tillandsia latifolia* (Ball Moss) from the Atacama Desert. It has stiff, spiny leaves arranged in a star-like fashion, but no roots. The plant forms a ball that rolls across the desert, blown by the wind. When conditions are moist, it absorbs moisture from the air.

Protection from the sun

Exposed to high-intensity sunlight, desert plants risk having their photosynthetic pigment (chlorophyll) damaged, and use various devices to combat this. Some cacti are covered in long white hairs that reflect much of the incoming radiation. Other species produce bulbous cells on their surfaces that shield the underlying photosynthetic cells and prevent the tissues becoming overheated. Air temperatures can exceed 131°F (55°C) during the day in many desert regions and leaf surfaces may become even hotter. At these high temperatures, vital biochemicals—such as the enzymes (proteins) that control many cell processes, including photosynthesis—may be damaged and rendered inactive. Only those plants whose proteins can cope with such extremes of heat can survive. One of the most tolerant plants is *Tidestromia oblongifolia* (Honeysweet), a native of western North America, which actually achieves its highest growth rate at temperatures of about 113°F (45°C).

M any of the types of plant that play an important part in the ecology of deserts are not so immediately evident as the shrubs and succulents. Among these are algae, lichens, fungi and short-lived annual and ephemeral flowering plants that spend much of the year hidden from view in one way or another.

Deserts might not appear to be promising habitats for mosses because they are so dry. Still, some species of moss, like those of the genus *Tortula*, are capable of survival, especially on rocky slopes and in crevices, where they receive some shelter from the direct sun. Mosses survive in the hot, dry conditions simply by drying out completely and becoming dormant until they are next provided with water. This often involves waiting an entire season and sometimes even several years. Such is the capacity of some of these plants to endure prolonged drought that dry specimens in museums have been known to recover and grow after 250 years without water. In addition, they can withstand temperatures as high as 131°F (55°C) while in a dry state.

Desert lichens

Even less conspicuous than the mosses, but far more widespread in deserts, are the lichens. Lichens are combinations of fungi and algae, or sometimes with blue-green bacteria (cyanobacteria). The algal cells live within the fungi, surrounded by a protective layer of fungal threads (called mycelia), which shade them from intense radiation and from desiccation. In return for this protective function, the fungus derives nutrition from the photosynthetic algae. The two live in mutually beneficial accord (symbiosis). An extra benefit for the fungus, when the photosynthetic member is a cyanobacterium, is nitrogen fixation: blue-green bacteria are able to convert nitrogen in the atmosphere into useable nitrogenous compounds. This can prove beneficial to the whole ecosystem. Lichens have no root system, but absorb water vapour from the atmosphere.

Lichens occur in a range of different forms. Some are projecting, leaf-like structures, others branching mats and some superficial crusts on rocks. These "crustose" lichens are extremely common on rocks in the desert wherever surface conditions are reasonably stable, but they are easily overlooked. Even less conspicuous than these superficial (epilithic) lichens are the lichens that live beneath a surface layer of rock (endolithic lichens), inhabiting the minute pores and crevices within the rock, especially in limestones. The living lichen occupies a layer up to

0.4 inches (1 centimeter) deep in the rock, where light still penetrates but where the delicate algal cells are protected from drying out. Probably the greatest problem that these rock-inhabiting lichens face is that the carbon dioxide they need from the air for photosynthesis reaches them only slowly.

Like the mosses, lichens become dry and dormant during unfavorable conditions and in this state they are extremely tolerant of both high and low temperature. The lichen *Ramalina maciformis*, for example, is not killed until the temperature reaches 185°F (85°C).

Short lives, long lives

Some desert plants are active only for limited periods. These are the annuals and ephemerals, including poppies, rockroses, grasses and chenopods. These plants spend most of the year (and most of their lives) as dormant seeds, only germinating under favorable conditions—when rain falls, for example. They then complete their life cycles very briefly, with a quick burst of flowering. Annuals and ephemerals devote most of their productivity to the formation of new seeds that will lie in dry soil until the next moist period. Mud bricks from archaeological sites have been found to contain seed that can still germinate after 300 years of internment. Some seeds also have to survive strong concentrations of salt.

Seed dispersal

Many of these plants have evolved special dispersal techniques to ensure that their seeds have the best possible chance to germinate. Some desert grasses, like the grass *Cenchrus biflorus* (known as *Cram-cram* in West Africa and *Heskanit* in Sudan) have seeds with sharp barbs, like velcro, which attach to clothing and fur, and are dispersed with them. Some early French geographers defined the edge of the real desert as the place where they noticed *cram-cram* on their socks. Other desert grasses produce a large number of seeds that become entangled, forming a ball shape that is easily blown through the desert. Individual seeds have sharp points that catch in the surface, detaching the seed from the ball. Eventually, the ball disintegrates, the seeds having been successfully dispersed.

▲ *"Living stones,"* or lithops, some of which are in flower. Originating from South Africa and Namibia, these plants grow partly underground, exposing only a small photosynthetic surface that resembles a rounded stone. As well as serving to conceal the plant from herbivores, the coloration also minimizes the temperature differential between the plant and its surroundings.

S urface area is important to desert invertebrates because the main route of water loss is through their surface. The smaller the organism, the greater its surface area relative to its volume. Not only this, they also have a smaller volume of fluid to start with. Water loss, therefore, becomes increasingly critical for smaller species, and many adaptations to the problem are found.

Following heavy rains in the desert, pools often form, providing a temporary source of water. These pools contain a surprising number of protozoa—very common, single-celled aquatic animals—including amoebae and ciliates. As the pools dwindle, these protozoa secrete a tough coating, or cyst, and survive in the soil in a dormant state until rain returns.

These temporary pools also frequently contain many crustaceans, including familiar marine invertebrates such as shrimps, lobsters, and crabs. Within a few days of their formation, desert pools can contain populations of small planktonic water fleas and cyclops. Within a week, the phyllopod *Triops* may be found. These animals grow to 1 inch (3 centimeters) in length and compete with tadpoles for the detritus in the water. *Triops* lays drought-resistant eggs before dying as the pools dry up.

Desert insects

Although they are small, insects have solved the water-loss problem by having a special waxy, waterproof layer to their cuticle (protective outer layer). This allows the insects to cope with desert life, and they are well represented in deserts, without having many further special adaptations.

Desert insects fall into two main groups. Many species fly, and this allows them to escape from the harshest conditions. After the rains, they can return to make use of the desert's resources. The other insect group is those that are poor fliers or have no ability to fly at all. They are permanent residents.

The desert locust (*Schistocerca gregaria*) is a powerful flier and migrates over vast areas of northern Africa and the Middle East. Like other locust species, *Schistocerca* periodically forms huge swarms that devastate vegetation, causing catastrophic losses to crops. Locusts are grasshoppers that herd together and move coherently. They exist in two forms, called solitary and gregarious. The solitary form

▼ **The banded gecko**
(Coleonyx variegatus)
is one of a great many
species of gecko that
inhabits desert regions.
It is nocturnal, hiding
under rocks during the
day and foraging for
insects at night.

of the desert locust looks and behaves quite differently from how it does when it has become the gregarious form. What induces the change from one form to another is thought to involve pheromones (airborne chemical messengers). If solitary individuals are crowded together they change to the gregarious form. Crowding occurs particularly when winds and rains converge. Distinctive winds ("low-level jets") associated with the monsoon bring the locusts together, and rains provide new plant growth to feed on and moist soil for egg laying. The population builds up locally and the switch from the solitary to the gregarious form takes place. The gregarious phase may then persist for several years until strong winds and storms disperse the swarm so that the isolated individuals revert to the solitary form.

Beetles are well suited to desert life. Scarab beetles (family Scarabaeidae) were revered by the ancient Egyptians, and were thought to represent life. Scarabs dispose of the dung of camels, goats, and donkeys by breaking off small portions, which they roll into balls and bury with an egg laid in each ball. Dung may also be buried and used as food store for adults. The tenebrionid beetle *Onymacris unguicularis* makes use of nighttime fog common in the Namib Desert. It adopts a curious "head down, bottom up" posture on the dune crests so that when the fog condenses on its body the water runs straight down to its mouth. There are many other "fog beetles" in other fog deserts, such as in Oman.

There are a number of predatory invertebrates. Centipedes, up to 8 inches (20 centimeters) long, use poisonous claws situated just behind their mouths to catch and kill prey. Scorpions' normal food consists of insects and spiders, which they grab with their large, crab-like chelae (pincers). They kill with an injection of venom from the sting at the end of their tail. Some of these venoms are potentially fatal, even to people. The solifugids, or camel spiders, are especially characteristic of African deserts. They have a pair of strong, vertically operating chelicerae (pincers) in front and use this to catch other invertebrates, lizards, mice, and even small birds.

▲ *The scarab beetle* (Dynastes hercules) *can grow up to 20 cm (8 in) and possesses a large horn that grows up to 10 cm (4 in) from its head.*

▼ *Scorpions of the family Buthidae, such as the species shown here, are among the few whose sting is potentially lethal to humans. Most scorpions are active at night and hunt mainly insects, although some of the larger species, which grow up to 19 cm (7.5 in) long, will attack rodents and small lizards.*

Gerbil
(Tatera indica).

Hyrax
(Procavia capensis).

▼ **Meerkats** (Suricata suricatta) *warming themselves in the morning sun. The upright stance improves their chances of spotting a predator.*

In the harsh desert environment, animals face three major, interrelated problems: high temperatures, shortage of food, and, above all, lack of water. Although deserts are so harsh, they are home to a surprisingly wide range of animal species, including many mammals. Large desert mammals include species like camels, donkeys, and goats, which have all been domesticated, but are all native to the desert or near-desert. There are also gazelles and the Arabian oryx (*Oryx leucoryx*), a threatened species. In the Namib Desert of coastal southern Africa, elephants and giraffes can also be found. In Australia, things are quite different. The placental mammals like those just described are absent, although the kangaroos, which are marsupials, have similar lifestyles to such animals as gazelles. Animals that are not native species, such as camels, have been introduced to the Australian desert. These are all herbivores, feeding on the sparse desert vegetation. Large predatory mammals are usually absent from deserts, although the Namib and Kalahari are exceptional in having some lions and jackals.

Smaller mammals include various ground squirrels, kangaroo rats, jerboas, gerbils and pocket mice. There are small carnivores, including the fennec fox (*Fennecus zerda*) in Africa and Arabia and the kit fox (*Vulpes velox*) in North America. In Australia there is the mulgara (*Dasycercus cristicauda*).

Coping with the heat

Animals of different sizes cope with high temperatures in different ways. Large mammals cannot escape the sun's heat as there is virtually no shade. Most have a thick coating of hair on their upper surface, which insulates the tissues beneath and keeps them relatively cool. The outer hair can reach very high temperatures: 158°F (70°C) has been recorded on the outside of a camel while the body temperature remained around 104°F (40°C). A light-colored coat helps to reflect some of the heat of the sun. While an animal's upper surface is well insulated, their undersurface, which is in shade, is often almost bare so that heat can easily be lost.

Fennec fox

Kit fox

▲ **The kit fox** (Vulpes velox) *and fennec fox* (Fennecus zerda) *are similar but unrelated desert mammals.*

Physiological adaptations allow many large mammals to tolerate an increase in body temperature. Mammals and birds are homoiotherms—that is they normally keep their body temperature constant. But some animals can adapt to heat by being able to tolerate a temperature rise. These animals can save on water that would otherwise be lost through sweating or panting. For instance, the body temperature of a camel may change more than 40°F (22°C) in a single day. During the cold night, the camel allows its body temperature to fall well below normal; during the day the sun warms the camel, past normal to a high of 106°F (41°C).

▼ **The addax** (Addax nasomaculatus) *is highly prized by hunters for its meat and skin.*

Small desert mammals deal with heat by avoiding it. They usually spend the daytime underground in burrows and emerge at night when it is cooler. Only a few species emerge briefly during the day, before returning to their burrows to cool off. The African ground squirrel (*Xerus erythropus*) uses its bushy tail as a parasol when it forages in the day. Desert rodents do not have sweat glands. In times of heat stress they dribble saliva onto their throat hair to cool themselves.

Saving water

With the exception of oases, there is little free drinking water available to desert mammals. However, given access to water, camels and donkeys can drink large amounts—between 20 and 25 percent of their body weight in a few minutes. Large mammals dig holes in dry riverbeds to reach water sources below the surface. Many animals lick or suck the dew and fog that condenses on plants.

▶ **The large ears** of the blacktailed jackrabbit (Lepus califoricus) contain a dense network of blood vessels that radiate away excess heat. Although expensive in energy, the rabbit's rapid, jumping style of locomotion minimizes the animal's contact with the hot, sun-baked surface and so reduces heat absorption.

▼ **An agile creature,** the common eland (Taurotragus oryx) is capable of huge leaps and of running at up to 25 mph (40 km/h). It has been successfully domesticated for its protein-rich milk and low-fat meat.

Much of the water that is taken in by desert animals comes from their food. Small, seed-eating mammals store seeds in their burrows. As the animals breathe, they exhale water vapor, which humidifies the air in the burrow. This moisture is then absorbed by the seeds and ultimately returns to the mammal when the seeds are eaten. Carnivores and insectivores meet their water needs through the body fluids of their prey.

Water is vitally important as a coolant, but it is also vital that the concentration of the body fluids remains constant; hence the mechanisms that allow temperatures to rise, which reduces the need to sweat or pant. But water is also lost, along with dissolved waste products, in urine. The kidneys control the water content of an animal's body. In desert mammals, particularly in smaller species, the region of the kidney, where water is reabsorbed from the urine, is enlarged. This allows these animals to produce very concentrated urine and so conserve water.

ADAPTING TO EXTREMES

Almost unbelievably, in a habitat characterized by a virtual absence of any standing water, both fish and amphibians are found in the deserts. In one of the hottest deserts on Earth, Death Valley on the Nevada-California border, several species of desert pupfish (*Cyprinodon* spp.) live in salty streams. The fish can tolerate temperatures as high as 111°F (43°C). On cold winter nights, these same fish also have to tolerate temperatures as low as 34 or 35°F (1 or 2°C). It is this considerable temperature tolerance, which is very unusual in aquatic animals, that has enabled the pupfish to survive in Death Valley for at least the last 30,000 years. These fish graze on blue-green algae, which are also highly tolerant of large temperature changes. Today the greatest threat to these tiny, uniquely hardy fish is not the harshness of the desert, but people. The growing demand for water in California is lowering the water table and some of the springs where the pupfish live are beginning to dry up.

▶ *The various species of desert pupfish are able to withstand huge temperature ranges. Despite this, pupfish will seek out the slightly cooler water temperatures afforded by niches.*

Reptiles and amphibians

Fish need permanent water, but amphibians need water only for breeding. Consequently, they can make use of temporary pools that form during occasional rainstorms. Amphibians normally lose water through their skins. However, desert species can tolerate a water loss of up to 50 percent of body weight. Some species retain dilute urine in a pouch of the digestive tract, rather than excreting it and losing the water.

Desert-dwelling amphibians, such as spadefoot toads (*Scaphiopus* spp.), pass the time between rains by aestivating. Aestivation is the hot-climate version of hibernation: the animal becomes dormant with a reduction in its energy needs. It is a technique used by many groups of desert animals to deal with periods of adverse conditions.

Among the mammals, ground squirrels aestivate, as do birds such as the poorwill (*Phalaenoptilus nuttallii*) and some reptiles. Aestivation usually occurs in seasons in which food or water is scarce. Spadefoot toads burrow down almost 3 feet (1 meter) into moist soil. Their outer skin layers then become harder and leathery to reduce water loss. In this situation, their metabolic rate drops dramatically, and they survive for up to nine months on fat reserves. With the onset of rain, the amphibians become active again, burrowing back to the surface and shedding their skin. Mating and egg-laying take place in freshly formed rainwater pools.

▼ *The spadefoot toad (Scaphiopus spp.) has adapted to life in dry climates. Its kidneys produce a concentrated solution of urea that can be released into its tissues in order to raise the concentration of the body fluids. The difference in concentration between the animal's body fluid and the surrounding soil causes water to enter the toad's body across its skin.*

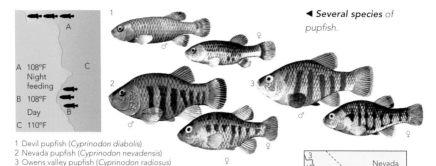

◀ *Several species* of pupfish.

1 Devil pupfish (*Cyprinodon diabolis*)
2 Nevada pupfish (*Cyprinodon nevadensis*)
3 Owens valley pupfish (*Cyprinodon radiosus*)

A 108°F
  Night
  feeding
B 108°F
  Day
C 110°F

Distribution of pupfish species around Death Valley

Compared with amphibians, reptiles are far more suited to desert life. Lizards, snakes, and tortoises all have thick, water-retentive skins. Most desert lizards and tortoises are diurnal (active during the day), while many of the snakes are nocturnal. In the summer, lizards usually avoid the hottest times of the day and are active in the morning the evening only, moving from light to shade to regulate temperature.

The desert tortoise in the Mojave Desert in California (*Gopherus agassizii*) is herbivorous, as are a few lizards. Most lizards and all snakes are carnivorous. Insects are the main food for smaller species, but the larger lizards and snakes feed on other lizards, rodents and eggs.

Desert birds

Perhaps just because they can fly, birds are common in deserts. Most are small. Birds have higher body temperatures than mammals, and can tolerate as much as 113°F (45°C) for long periods of time. Most desert birds reduce activity during the heat of the day, since this would elevate their body temperature.

In the absence of trees, many nests are on the ground. Eggs can be buried by sand or become over-heated if left uncovered for any period of time and there is always the possibility of the eggs being eaten.

The bird equivalent of the camel is the ostrich (*Struthio camelus*). This large flightless bird is usually found in sizable herds, mainly in southern Africa, although it was once common in Northern Africa and even Arabia. Its fine feathers provide a thick insulation against the Sun. By drooping the wings, the sparsely feathered, thoracic region is shaded and can radiate excess heat. Like other birds, ostriches cannot sweat to keep cool. If heat-stressed, the ostrich pants, losing water vapor from its throat, so cooling the body.

▼ *Africa is the home of* the ostrich, the largest living bird. It is the only member of the order Struthioniformes. The ostrich runs to escape its predators and can reach speeds of up to 40 mph (65 km/h).

THE DESERT ECOSYSTEM

The desert ecosystem is a community of living organisms interacting with its non-living environment. The energy from the sun fuels photosynthesis and the organic matter of plants provides energy for herbivores, which are themselves preyed upon by other animals. Carbon dioxide gas, and nitrates from the soil are taken up by plants and made into living organic matter. When dead organisms are consumed by fungi and bacteria, many of their component molecules are released into the non-living world.

Energy input

The input of energy into the desert ecosystem comes from the photosynthetic production of new plant material. The rate of this "production" in deserts is generally low—very similar to the rate in arctic tundra (hence the definition of deserts as places with little vegetation). The growth in plant material is erratic and depends on the availability of water. The production of new plant material may fail completely if there is prolonged drought, but the minimum amount of precipitation needed for plant growth varies. The North American hot desert ecosystems, for example, need 1.5 inches (38 millimeters) of annual precipitation to maintain the growth of perennial plants, but in the Namib Desert

▼ *A variety of* **animals,** *including a giraffe, ostriches, and eland, gather at a waterhole in Skeleton Coast Park, Namibia. Waterholes are the most favourable habitats in the whole of the desert ecosystem and attract a wide variety of visitors over great distances. However, the scarcity of food resources means that permanent residents are few.*

an annual grass, *Stipagrostis gonatostacys*, is able to grow when precipitation is as low as 0.4 inch (10 millimeters) per year.

The energy fixed from sunlight by plants is available to grazing animals, ranging from grasshoppers, bugs and aphids, to gerbils, ostriches, and oryx. Not all the energy finds its way into the consumers, however. Some is used by the plants, or is lost when plants die.

Food webs

The feeding relationships of animals in the desert, as in other ecosystems, are very complex and form a food web in which there are different levels of feeding ("trophic levels"). Animals may occupy several different positions, depending on what food is available. Because the passage of energy from one trophic level to the next is relatively inefficient, especially in deserts, there are usually smaller numbers of animals (and lower biomass—the total mass of living things) at each succeeding level. Within the ecosystem, interactions between different components often lead to predictable, cyclic processes. A wet period may lead to a burst of vegetative production and an explosion in the population of invertebrate grazers. This may be followed by a build-up of predators and scavengers.

Vegetation and the environment

Vegetation has a considerable effect on the physical environment, creating patches of shade, reducing windspeeds and protecting the soil surface from the effects of rain impaction, surface runoff, and wind erosion. Even a lichen crust has an important role in surface stabilization, because it protects the soil from the rain or wind and absorbs much of the moisture, reducing surface runoff. The vegetation cover as a whole reflects the Sun's rays and creates a thermal blanket, which prevents the surface from becoming excessively hot and so modifies the movement of water in the soil. The removal of plant cover by overgrazing and fuel-wood collection can, for these reasons, lead to degradation.

▲ *An elf owl*
(Micrathene whitneyi) *perches on a cactus in the Sonoran Desert of southwest United States. Growing to 5.5 in (14 cm) in length, this small owl feeds on insects, and the occasional mouse or lizard. If caught by a larger predator, the elf owl will play dead until the threat has passed.*

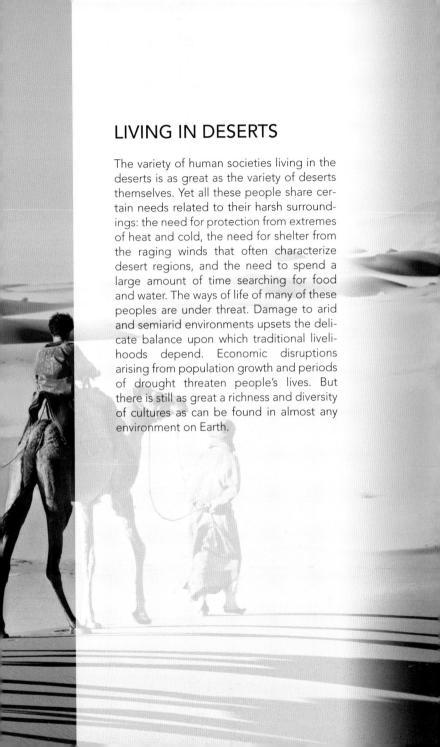

LIVING IN DESERTS

The variety of human societies living in the deserts is as great as the variety of deserts themselves. Yet all these people share certain needs related to their harsh surroundings: the need for protection from extremes of heat and cold, the need for shelter from the raging winds that often characterize desert regions, and the need to spend a large amount of time searching for food and water. The ways of life of many of these peoples are under threat. Damage to arid and semiarid environments upsets the delicate balance upon which traditional livelihoods depend. Economic disruptions arising from population growth and periods of drought threaten people's lives. But there is still as great a richness and diversity of cultures as can be found in almost any environment on Earth.

DESERT PEOPLES

The earliest known remains and artefacts of what are considered to be true humans have been found in desert regions, particularly those of East Africa. These regions were not, however, deserts at the times from which these finds date. Nonetheless, some of the earliest human cultures did exist in these same regions after they had become desert.

Desert peoples, particularly those of the Nile, the Tigris-Euphrates and the Indus river valleys, were also responsible for creating the first agricultural economies, characterized by the development of settled, irrigated farming. Similar economic revolutions took place in the high deserts of South America and in the southwestern United States.

Culture and religion

The core of the world's most extensive desert region, the Sahara and the neighboring parts of Asia, is closely associated with the Semitic people, particularly the Arabs. They now are the main group living in a majority in countries of the Middle East. Other ethnic groups, however, do exist in the region. In the North African countries of Morocco, Algeria, Tunisia and Libya, for example there are significant Berber populations. On the southern side of the Sahara most peoples are of African origin, but over the last 1,000 years their distinctive character has been modified by longstanding connections with the peoples of the northern Sahara. The deserts of southern Africa have become a refuge for the traditional peoples of the Kalahari and the Namib deserts.

▶ *A San hunter* of *Botswana takes aim with traditional hunting bow and poison-tipped arrow. The San, together with the Khoi-khoin, form the Khoisan group, whose homeland is in southern Africa. Like the Australian Aborigines, the Khoisan have an ancient desert culture, which is carefully adapted to their hostile environment.*

◀ *Situated 12 mi*
(20 km) south of the city
of Al Minya in Egypt
lies the village of Bani
Hassan al Shurruq. The
village is home to some
390 tombs, the interiors
of which are decorated
with scenes from the
Middle Kingdom of
ancient Egypt.

The majority of the peoples of the arid regions of the Central Asian republics, as well as the dry areas of Turkey, are Turkic in origin and culture. In the Gobi Desert, most people are Khalkha Mongols. The geographical positions of these deserts, however, has meant that their populations have often been exposed to influences and migrations from many surrounding areas.

Outside the Old World, many desert areas were settled by Europeans during the 19th century and the first part of the 20th century, usually displacing or subjecting the original population. In North America, the original desert peoples of the southwest, such as the Navajo and Apache, were deprived of their land by European intruders. They were dispersed or relocated and their numbers severely reduced. Since that time, there has been a massive migration of settlers into the Sun Belt states from the multiethnic population of the contemporary United States. Large numbers of the descendants of the original Mexican people and those of mixed Mexican-Spanish origin live in the deserts of Mexico.

The mountain deserts of the Andes of South America are inhabited by the descendants of the Indian peoples who civilized the region during the past 1,000 years. The Atacama Desert of South America is such an extreme environment that the populations there have always been small; significant settlement has only been recorded in the modern era.

The Aborigines of arid Australia were severely reduced in numbers during the European invasion of the 1800s onward. Some were displaced from their homes and cultural sites to make way for mineral exploitation.

Modern deserts

All the deserts of the world have much higher populations today than at any time in the past. This is particularly true of the deserts of North America and Australia, where major urban centers and some large cities – Phoenix, Tucson, Salt Lake City, and even Los Angeles – exist in arid regions. Mining and agricultural development attracted settlement in a few of the dry tracts of Australia, while in the Middle East, oil exploration and subsequent development have caused substantial urban and industrial centers to blossom. The origins of the people employed to construct and then live in these new population centers are often very diverse. There are millions of people from the south and southeast of Asia living in cities sited on the very arid coasts of the Gulf region. Dubai is an emblematic example.

Today's desert margins contain a great deal of evidence of traditional societies and cultures, but almost everywhere the lifestyles of their populations are closely integrated into the modern world. In addition, because many economic activities in the world's deserts provide high mineral- and oil-derived revenues, the international community takes a great deal of interest in the economic and strategic affairs of these regions. A consequence is that the communities who reside there are often very international indeed. Dry desert margins with little vegetation place great demands on the ingenuity of the peoples who live in them. In hot semiarid regions, the need is to insulate people—and where possible livestock—from the extreme midday heat. It is also necessary to ensure that living spaces are ventilated and that air circulation and cooling breezes are as effective as possible. There is an additional challenge in areas that endure cold winter nights. In cold deserts, the main need is still insulation, but from the cold, especially from the extreme cold of winter.

▼ *Two Bedouin* *tribesman* use a laptop computer and mobile phone. Even ancient desert cultures have embraced new communications technology for a variety of reasons.

Materials for construction are scarce in both hot and cold deserts. As a result, some of the earliest dwellings were caves, and there is widespread evidence of this from the Mesolithic and Neolithic periods in the Sahara and in the Middle Eastern deserts. In northern Africa, natural caverns were enlarged and in a few places were used until the very recent past. Similar dwellings were created in the dry areas of what is now the southwestern United States.

Materials for the construction of permanent and temporary shelter have, throughout the human settlement of desert margins, come from the ground, plants, and animals. Deserts are rich in rock cover and in some place also in clay deposits. Hides, wool, and animal hair are relatively abundant in relation to the small human populations of deserts, although the supply of useful vegetation is often poor. Permanent dwellings traditionally were built with mud brick and brick in areas where clay occurs. River valleys have provided readily accessible material for the manufacture of sun-baked mud bricks, and later for kiln-fired bricks. During the major ancient civilizations that graced the semiarid regions of the world, the excavation and the transport of massive quantities of ambitiously engineered and skillfully dressed stone became important industries as the towns and cities of these early civilizations grew.

There have been urban centers in the world's desert margins from the earliest times, but the deep deserts can be inhabited only by people who adopt a mobile lifestyle that enables them to use the scarce fodder and water of the remote desert tracts. These people need either portable or temporary shelter. Tents made either from cloth or animal skins have been the main type of transportable shelter used by nomadic desert peoples for the past 10,000 years. The *ger*, a hut made of cloth stretched over a wooden frame, is widely used by the nomads of Central Asia. Temporary shelter can be constructed very easily where there are shrubs and trees from which woody material can be collected.

Modern shelter

High technology has transformed the options available to modern desert dwellers. Artificial climates can be created in efficiently insulated structures with effective ventilation and air conditioning. The temporary nature of the traditional tent is emulated in the modern air-conditioned trailer. Such dwellings are not used by traditional livestock rearers, but largely for transient mineral and oil exploration camps. The numerous and rapidly developing permanent settlements of the oil-rich Gulf and of the Sun Belt of the United States have attracted many of the world's best architects.

SHELTER: THE ISLAMIC TRADITION

In Islamic architecture, the style of the construction of dwellings depends on several factors: the physical environment including water supply, temperature, wind and rainfall, and cultural elements, such as social patterns and the strictures of religion. In addition, the Islamic tradition influences the development of individual house style and structure in urban settlements.

To illustrate the development of Islamic urban settlements and houses suitable for hot semiarid and arid environments, we can take Iran as an example. There are some religious and social factors unique to Iran that have influenced the way in which houses there have developed. The elements of construction influenced by the requirements of climate and the physical environment, however, are reflected in other desert regions of the Islamic world—and in some non-Islamic areas.

Urban development and the physical environment

In Iran, in a way typical of arid countries, cities have grown up largely in areas with an accessible water supply and sufficient irrigable land for the needs of the population. The main source of water in the region is from artificial subterranean channels, the *qanats*, which govern the distribution of urban settlements. *Qanat* systems that surround the great northern salt desert of Iran, for example, reflect the urban developments that encircle the plain. Another factor is the winds that characterize the area and which restrict the use of the plains for agriculture or settlement. Political and strategic (military or other) demands also influence the position of urban centers.

Modern cities in Iran are increasingly built without taking climatic conditions into account. Such cities are made possible by the use of very large amounts of energy to drive the equipment needed to make them habitable, such as air conditioning systems and water pumps.

The design of houses

The usual pattern of a house is a central open courtyard surrounded on two or three sides by rooms. Houses are built in a cell structure, that is, sharing walls with neighboring buildings, usually on three sides, leaving the fourth side facing on to the street. The walls are normally thick, made with layers of clay or mud bricks, to restrict the conduction of heat into the house. The ground in the courtyard area is often somewhat below the level of the street to increase the amount of shade and to help retain cooler night air during the day and so reduce temperature inside the house.

▲ **Multistory** town houses at Shibām in southern Yemen are among the most spectacular examples of mud-brick architecture, and represent a 1,000-year urban tradition. Most of the houses are built out of mud bricks, and many date back to the 16th century. The town is a UNESCO World Heritage site.

High walls that run around the courtyard add to this effect.

Traditional houses, particularly those in the richer quarters, have a pool or even a fountain in the courtyard, again serving to reduce the temperature inside the house. Also largely restricted to richer householders is the construction of a garden in the courtyard. A garden could be used to provide additional food, but its primary use, beyond the purely decorative, is to cool the house. Internal gardens are not only found in private buildings: mosques and other public structures, particularly those from the medieval period, often have garden courtyards.

Even in the poorer quarters of traditional Iranian cities, houses often include north-facing rooms that are designed for use during the hotter months. These rooms often hold another pool of water—in addition to the courtyard pool.

Unique to Iran, and of particular interest to the modern architect attempting to reduce reliance on artificial air-cooling systems, is the *bad-gir*, or wind-catcher. The *bad-gir* is a tower rising from the summer room and reaching to about 60 feet (20 meters) above ground. The tower has two sets of vents at the top: one smaller set facing the prevailing wind, and a larger set facing away. Relatively cool wind is channelled into the tower. The greater density of the cool air causes it to sink down into the house, while the less dense warm air inside the building rises to the rear vent and is expelled. The downward air is often cooled further by channelling it over a pool or through a filter of damp leaves.

Extremes of winter climate on the desert margins lead the more affluent householders to build winter quarters. These are on the south side of the house in order to benefit from the heat absorbed by the walls from the winter sun. As might be expected, doorways and air channels are smaller than in the summer quarters, and the circulation of air is further restricted by textile coverings over the door and windows.

CLOTHING

The clothing of peoples of the desert margins depends largely on the temperatures of the desert where they live. The Australian Aboriginals, for example, originally wore only loincloths, and sometimes dispensed even with these. Their naturally dark skin pigmentation is sufficient to protect them from the Sun, while temperatures at night are rarely low enough to warrant clothing. If temperatures did drop, Aborigines would use fur blankets. The nomadic herdsmen of the Tibet deserts, on the other hand, wear robes with long sleeves and high collars, along with a sheepskin hat and perhaps a woollen or sheepskin wrap to protect them from the cold that prevails in their high-altitude environment.

Clothing must be durable, not only because of the scarcity of materials, but also because the crafts involved in creating materials for clothing are very labor-intensive. Many of the desert dwellers of the Americas, such as the Pueblo, Navajo, and Inca peoples, for example, took great pride in their handwoven garments. The Pueblo, in particular, were highly skilled at weaving and making cotton clothes, some of which were exceptionally colorful. They spun yarn from cotton and turned it into cloth. The men wore cotton breeches

▼ *The headgear* worn by Tuareg men protects them from both desert winds and sand, as well as from evil spirits that lurk in dark, lonely places. The indigo robes worn by the Tuareg have given them the name "blue men of the desert;" however, the Tuareg refer to themselves simply as "Kel Tagilmust," or "people of the veil."

▲ **The clothing** of desert peoples is usually fairly dark. Such colors have the best insulating properties and desert dust shows up least against earthern hues.

and kilts, and the women dressed in cotton wraps. Around their legs, both the men and women wore buckskin leggings. Later, when the Spanish introduced sheep, the Pueblo Indians also made woolen clothes. Other tribes of southwest America, particularly the Navajo and Apache peoples, originally wore skins from the animals they hunted, but their increased interaction with the Pueblo encouraged them to make cloth.

Clothing and culture

Among the cultures that used clothing, the designs were often closely associated with the religion of the area. In the vast semiarid regions where Islam originated, for example, similar basic designs occur over very extensive areas. In the regions where Muslim tradition has been a strong influence, the conventions of modesty and cleanliness prevail. Figurative display is absent and geometric Arabesque decoration is preferred on artifacts as well as clothing. The personal modesty required by the religion and culture of many of the desert margin peoples, especially those of Asia and the Middle East, reinforces the tendency to cover the body to protect it from the heat, and it is common in Muslim countries to cover the whole body, including the head.

Headgear is distinguishing feature of male members of the nomadic groups of Arabia and northern Africa, and women also often wear distinguishing headdresses. The veil for women is not, however, common among nomadic peoples, and women members of many such tribes participate freely and without constraint in the economy and daily life of their communities. Footwear is easily created from the skins of the livestock, and sandals of simplicity and considerable elegance have long been, and remain, a part of the normal dress of the peoples of the desert margins, although going barefoot for long periods is also common. The surface in semiarid regions can become uncomfortably hot to the feet after many hours and the protection of the sandal is often essential if distances have to be covered at hot periods.

73

FOOD AND NUTRITION

The range and volume of foods that are naturally available to peoples living on the margins of the world's deserts are severely restricted by the availability of water. Because of the intrinsic environmental uncertainty of arid and semiarid regions, nutrition in deserts and their margins, for both human and animal populations, has always been unreliable and often poor.

In the Middle Eastern and North African semi-arid regions, only livestock rearing and some oasis agriculture are possible. These activities yield a limited range of products: meat, milk, blood and their derivatives, dates and some vegetables, but no staple grains. Therefore diets rich in animal proteins and fats, such as sheep, goat, and camel meat, as well as poultry and eggs, are common, although products from cattle are usually scarce. Pork products are generally forbidden by religion in these regions. Dates are rich in sugar, but diets generally are poor in the starchy carbohydrates and fiber that are derived from bread, because grain is difficult to cultivate.

At the desert margins, conditions are less extreme than in the desert cores, and diets are consequently less austere. However, diets are also less stable here because of the great variations in rainfall that occur from year to year. Livestock numbers rise and fall in response to the seasonal and yearly changes in the availability of fodder, which is in turn a reflection of changeable rainfall patterns. Variations in rainfall also affect the "catch" crops of grain or vegetables, which are raised when rains permit. The earliest domestic grain production, probably of barley and later of wheat, can be traced to the desert margins of the Middle East and North Africa 11,000 years ago.

▲▼ **Grown today** as an ornament as well as for its fruit, the date palm (Phoenix dactylifera) has been cultivated for more than 4,000 years. The fruit is often dried.

Lifestyle and food

The lifestyles and economic strategies forced on desert peoples are, in general, centered around the continual necessity to insure against food shortage and to preserve what foodstuffs are available. However, in some of the world's desert countries, oil revenues have transformed consumption options as international trade brings in products from all over the world. Since the 1930s, desert areas in industrialized countries, such as those in the southwest of the United States, have been transformed through the use of irrigation systems into some of the world's major

▲ Sudanese women
pounding maize outside their tents. Brought back from the New World by the Spanish before the end of the 15th century, maize was introduced into Africa by the Portuguese in the early 16th century. Within a generation the new crop had spread throughout Africa, in many cases supplanting Old World cereals such as barley and millet.

food exporting economies. The people of these areas enjoy a diet as varied and as privileged as any in the world. Similarly, Saudi Arabia has also become a significant desert food producer, using its fossil groundwater resources to irrigate food and fodder crops.

In the absence of such opportunities, nomadism has been the major economic strategy for millennia. Food shortages often follow poor rains, and a mobile way of life allows the desert communities and their economies to be responsive to the ever-changing quality of food supplies. The inherent mobility of this lifestyle means that bulky, heavy food and water supplies cannot be moved about.

The preservation of food is a preoccupation of desert peoples because it is so scarce. Fat and sugar are the main preservatives, and for the most part they are readily available in the desert economy. In the dry desert air, fruit, meat, and fish are all easy to preserve, making proteins, carbohydrates, and sugars available over long periods. Salt is another important preservative, and occurs naturally in many locations as a result of evaporation.

TOOLS AND IMPLEMENTS

Inhabitants of the desert live in some of the very harshest environments in the world. Those of the Middle Eastern deserts have to cope with searing daytime temperatures followed by freezing nights. Conditions in the semiarid regions of northern Asia vary dramatically over the course of one year. In the Gobi Desert, winter temperatures can be as low as –40°F (–40°C) and summer temperatures can soar to as high as 113°F (45°C). In addition, the quality of desert soil is usually very poor and sometimes, as is the case in parts of the Gobi Desert, there is no soil. The lack of soil, even if water were to be available, makes it impossible to grow crops or graze livestock. The major problem that is common to all peoples of the desert is, of course, the scarcity of water.

Traveling light

The sparseness of vegetation and the extreme seasonal changes determine the strategies of hunter-gathering and agricultural and pastoral nomadism as the only feasible premodern ways of surviving. For nomads, all possessions must be easily portable. This not only disciplines nomads against accumulating possessions in the first place, it also ensures that those possessions that they do have are light or disposable. The Australian Aborigines of arid areas, perhaps out of all desert peoples, traveled the lightest. They usually moved only in small family groups and required little shelter. To protect themselves from the strong winds that sweep the Australian deserts, Aborigines made windbreaks from saplings covered with brush or bark. If it became suddenly cold, they would sleep close to their domesticated dingoes for warmth. When traveling, the men carried simple weapons for hunting, such as spears and boomerangs, while the women carried deep wooden bowls in which to collect fruits and berries. In some areas, plaited or painted bark baskets were

▼ *An elderly man* works on a camel saddle with traditional tools outside a shed in the Indian desert town of Jaisalmer.

carried for gathering, and kangaroo-skin water bags were used in very arid areas.

For the San (or Bushmen) of the Kalahari, a long stick sharpened at one end was used to dig up the roots and tubers that, together with berries and fruits, made up a large part of their diet. While women were responsible for gathering berries and roots, hunting was the preserve of the men. A light bow with poison-tipped arrows was used to kill antelope and small desert mammals.

The nomadic tribes of the Middle East and Asia, compared to the Australian Aborigines or the San, travel in larger groups and need greater protection from the elements. The sparse or nonexistent vegetation of the Middle East and Asian semiarid regions, however, provides few raw materials for the requirements of their inhabitants. In most of these deserts, for example, wood is scarce except for the trunks of palm trees, and even these have few of the qualities of temperate or tropical timbers. Grass and reeds are available in abundance in the river valleys, but these are accessible to only a limited number of these desert dwellers. A few drought-resistant grass species grow in the desert margins and these are available to a more substantial proportion of the desert population. These materials are sometimes used to make objects in which to store and carry food. Although some drought-resistant shrubs are used to make shelters, it is more common for camels, goats, yaks and sheep to provide a source of fibers and skins with which desert dwellers construct their tents.

Changing ways

Modern economic systems and the engineering, building, and transport systems associated with them have also had a very strong effect on the lives of the peoples living in the deserts of Africa, Asia, and the Middle East. The proportions of the populations deriving livelihoods from the desert tracts through nomadic practices have fallen dramatically since the 1950s. At that time, many countries of the Middle East and North Africa, such as Saudi Arabia, the Emirates of the Gulf, and Libya, had more than 20 percent of their populations living as nomads. By 1990, the proportions were less than three percent and the numbers were constantly falling. The places where the craft and creative traditions have survived are those regions where oil revenues have not had a determining effect on local economies. It is in Yemen, in Iran, in some parts of Turkey, in Afghanistan, and in the deserts of Central Asia that the traditional ways of life and crafts of the desert peoples can still be found to a significant degree.

CUSTOMS AND RELIGION

Many people think of Islam as the religion predominantly associated with deserts. Islam is discussed overleaf, but there are of course many desert regions where Islam is not the predominant religion.

In South America, old traditions often mix with new beliefs, and so, for example, Catholicism with an influence from pre-Columbian Inca beliefs characterizes the religion of Peru today. In North America, before the arrival of the Europeans, shamanistic belief systems dominated the desert regions, as they did most other parts of the continent. After the arrival of Europeans, Christianity again came to dominate the region, although some traditions remained and became absorbed into the new religion.

In Australia, the Aborigines have a rich and varied set of totemic beliefs. In such religions there is a close relationship between a person or group and some natural object or phenomenon, as well as a kinship between people and nature.

Asia and North Africa

In arid Asian regions, such as Mongolia, Ladakh, or Mustang, Buddhism established itself at an early date, taking the Tibetan Lamaist form. In the Middle East, in outlying areas of Syria, Kurdistan, and the Caucasus, the Nusayris, the Yezidis, and the Ali-Ilahis have retained customs and beliefs that originated in various cults that characterized the settled Middle Eastern peoples in ancient times. Many of these cults were associated with agriculture, irrigation, and a belief in a Mother Goddess, but the desert, too, housed important centers where, it was believed, the gods had their temples. Two of these places were caravan centers: Petra in Jordan and Palmyra in Syria.

Similar gods and goddesses, and similar types of temples, characterized the beliefs of the early Arabs in the Yemen, in southern Arabia. Zoroastrianism was the national religion of the ancient Persians and prevailed in the region until most followers converted to Islam in the 7th century CE. However, there are still many Zoroastrians

▼ *The unmistakable symbol of Buddhism, the eight-spoked wheel of life. Buddhism is the major religion of many desert regions in Asia, and was spread via the Silk Route, much of which crosses vast arid areas.*

in Iran. The founder of the religion, Zoroaster (born 588 BCE), who conceived of a cosmic struggle between the powers of Good and Evil, was born in the desert region of Chorasmia, bordering on Khorasan, Afghanistan, and Turkmenia.

Judaism was a desert religion when the Israelites wandered in the wilderness. Around the date of the birth of Christ, the Jewish sect of the Essenes, and likeminded men such as John the Baptist and "eaters of locusts and wild honey," settled in the Wilderness of Judea near the Dead Sea. Their settlement of Qumran is now well known because of the discovery of the Dead Sea Scrolls nearby.

Christianity in Egypt and Nubia became famous for its desert monks and ascetics, and for the establishment of monasteries of the Coptic church. The monks in Wadi Natrun are there to this day, whereas the monastery of St Catherine at the foot of Mount Sinai is all but abandoned. Several desert monasteries were founded in the Judean wilderness outside Jerusalem. At Kilwa, now in the remote Tubayq region of Saudi Arabia, there is a tiny 6th-century settlement of monks.

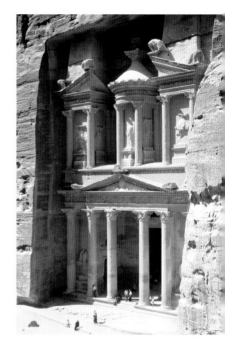

▲ *A rock-cut façade* at Petra, the "rose red city, half as old as time itself." The inhabitants of Petra had their own religion, but were influenced by classical Greek architecture and aesthetics. The elaborate features of the façade, including the decorated pillars, were all patiently carved from the natural cliff face. Inside the cliff are several small chambers.

Apart from the Arabs, it is the Turkic peoples who have dominated the desert regions of Central Asia. Archaeology has shown how mixed were the earlier beliefs of the people of the desert steppes of Central Asia. Excavations at the site of medieval Taraz (Dzhambul in Kazakhstan) reveal that in the medieval period the surrounding towns professed Zoroastrianism, Christianity, and Buddhism. The region had local cults: a Bacchic cult, a cult of the fertility goddess Anahit, and a Turkic cult of heaven. There were also believers in the Manichaen religion, an eclectic offshoot of Zoroastrianism.

Nevertheless, it was the Turkish shaman, a "medicine man" who assisted the people to maintain the delicate balance between the world of pragmatic necessity and the unseen world of the spirits, who was at the heart of many of the customs and beliefs of the ancient Turks. The religions that later came to dominate the desert regions of Central Asia were deeply influenced by shamanistic beliefs. This was true of Islam; the beliefs became a marked part of the rituals of the mystical movements and orders, such as the Sufis. Many of these orders originated in the desert areas of Central Asia.

ISLAM

Islam is the dominant religion of the desert stretches of the Middle East and North Africa. Of the pre-Islamic customs that have continued in these areas, some have been absorbed into Islamic practice. Examples include the cult of saints and the belief in superhuman forces, variously termed jinn, ifrit, or ghul. These beings are said to inhabit deserted ruins, mountainous rocky outcrops, or solitary trees that have miraculously survived in the wilderness. To the ancient Arabs these trees were sacred. The "burning bush" that Moses, who is himself recognized by Islam as a prophet, encountered in the Sinai Desert may have been one such tree.

A nomadic religion?

The close relationship between many pre-Islamic customs and Islam itself has prompted the assertion that Islam was a religion born in the desert, a religion that reflected a nomadic mentality. Some historians, however, deny this. They argue that the Prophet Muhammad, the founder of Islam, was a citizen of Makkah (Mecca), a thriving city supporting a rich merchant class that had little in common with nomadic peoples, and that therefore the desert and its people had little, if any, creative part in the origin of Islam. However, it is also important to remember that it was the same merchant class that opposed Muhammad, eventually forcing him and his followers to leave Makkah and travel to al Medina, where he set up his new religious community. The city of Makkah, however, remains the religious center for all Muslims. For those Muslims who can afford it, a pilgrimage to Makkah is something that should be undertaken at least once in a lifetime.

Whether or not Islam was born directly out of the desert, the well, the oasis, and the mirage furnish much of the imagery of the oral and written literature of Muslim peoples, from Qingjiang to the Atlantic shore.

In the desert, religion and culture are shaped by the environment. Towns are few and

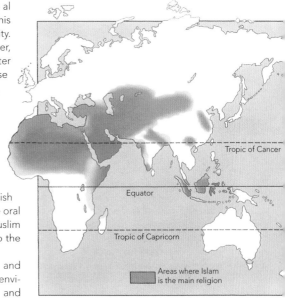

▼ **Islam** is the world's fastest-growing religion with some 1.3 billion adherents. From the early 7th century to the mid-8th century CE, Islam spread rapidly from the Arabian Peninsula into Persia, North Africa, and Spain. Islam then suffered a series of setbacks, but by the 13th century Islam had spread into India, and over the next two centuries large areas of Africa and Southeast Asia were to join the Muslim world.

Tropic of Cancer

Equator

Tropic of Capricorn

Areas where Islam is the main religion

where congregational mosques exist, for example in Tombouctou (Timbuktu) in Mali or Bukhoro in Uzbekistan, they are substantial structures made of stone or from mud brick. In open desert, many mosques are simple lines of stones indicating the direction of Makkah. In Central Asia, in the area of former nomadism, there are holy places that are related to the Islamic mystic (Sufi) brotherhoods, to the cult of ancestors (in Turkmenistan), or to pre-Islamic sanctuaries (in Kyrghyzstan) that have since assumed an Islamic mantle. Sometimes they are situated amid Muslim cemeteries. These are not only places for prayer but also, at certain seasons, sites for nomadic fairs and markets.

Islam versus custom

The life of the nomad, whether Arab, Tuareg, Fulani, or Somali, follows a strict pattern based around birth, circumcision, marriage, and death, interspersed with seasonal feasts, which are often celebrated with a hospitality shown to both relative and guest. In the desert, women are often freer in many respects than they are in villages or cities and there are strong matrilineal features among the Tuareg, the Moors, and some of the Tartars. Among the Tuareg, lineage even stems from maternal ancestors.

Often in desert Islamic communities there is a class who form "clerical tribes." The members of this class live in remote areas, teaching the Qur'an in tented schools, curing the sick with amulets, or prescribing remedies that are derived from desert herbs. Their supreme duty is to pray for rain, because the survival of the nomads and their herds of camels, sheep, and, in Sahelian regions, cattle lies in the coming of the rainclouds.

Nomadic custom centers around loyalty to the patrilineal (or matrilineal) tribe. This adherence transcends even loyalty to Islam. The great heroes of the desert Arabs, such as Abu Zayd of the Bani Hilal, were prepared to kill and die for their tribe's survival. Abu Zayd crossed the deserts of North Africa to find pasturage for his famished people. Unseen voices guided the hero to his destination. The code of hospitality that makes a nomad's life of less value than that of his guest has a potentially negative counterpart that takes the form of requirement for revenge if the honor of the tribe is at stake. Another area of potential conflict between religious and social duty is that whereas Islam has tried to establish a community of the faithful, custom requires the absolute loyalty of tribal members to fight for the survival of the tribe, its herds, and the retention of its pasturage.

TOWNS AND CITIES

People were slow to build settlements in the deserts. The earliest communities faced the major problem of finding reliable water supplies for drinking and cultivation. Sometimes, because of their extreme isolation and difficult access, desert settlements were built as refuges for people who had been driven from more fertile lands by invaders.

In the Nile Valley, Mesopotamia, the Iranian Plateau, and the Lower Indus Valley, settlement began 6,000 years ago. The Egyptian and Mesopotamian settlements depended on efficient irrigation systems that, along with the fertile soil, brought in huge harvests. Soon, in areas such as those around Edfu and Luxor on the banks of the Nile, there evolved a sophisticated urban culture. Other cities flourished in desert conditions in and around the Nile Delta. The fabulous cities of Ur and Babylon grew up in Mesopotamia, and Mohenjo-Daro and Harappa arose in what is now Pakistan. Urban life has continued in Egypt ever since, despite occasional political and economic upheavals. Settlements in Mesopotamia, however, foundered through soil salinization, although what are now Baghdad and Damascus have remained important centers of population throughout most of the historic period.

The early Persians used river water and underground canal (*qanat*) systems to support large desert towns. The empires of Cyrus and Darius, for example, evolved in the arid plateaux of the Iranian Desert at sites such as Parsagard and Persepolis. Although between 336 and 330 BCE these centers were destroyed by Greek and Arab invaders, Alexander the Great set up governorates (satrapies) in outlying areas within the Persian Empire, which maintained an Irano-Greek urban form for many centuries after his death. Balkh in the Turkestan Desert of Central Asia is an example of one such governorate. The Mogul emperors in India, similarly, took forms of Persian urban culture to desert areas of India, notably the Thar Desert of the northwest.

The influence of Islam

With the rise of Islam in the 7th century CE, Makkah and Al Madina became important centers of pilgrimage in the Arabian Desert, which until that time had lacked significant settlements. Islam not only revitalized many towns and cities in both the Nile and Tigris-Euphrates valleys and elsewhere in the desert lands of North Africa, and Middle East and South Asia; it also played an important part in the development of new towns such as El Qahir (Cairo), Marrakech and Fès (Fez), with their elegant minarets, mosques, universities, palaces, bazaars, and city squares. Today, North African, Middle East-

▼ *The Cliff Palace* is an ancient Anasazi cultural settlement in Chapin Mesa, at Mesa Verde National Park, Colorado. These houses were built of rock and adobe (sun-dried bricks) between 1,000 and 800 years ago. The cliff overhang provides an easily defensible location that is also protected from the elements. Today, the Hopi people, descendants of the Anasazi, live in similar communities.

ern, and south Asian areas remain some of the most densely populated desert regions anywhere in the world.

Before the Arabs, very few cities grew up in the deep Sahara. Small settlements such as Ghudamis and Marzūq were all that could survive on limited water supplies in so hostile an environment. The semiarid Mediterranean fringes of the Sahara, however, supported magnificent early cities.

The invasion by the Arabs of North Africa in the early centuries of Islam created a new series of towns in the mountain rims of the Sahara in North Africa. They were populated by Berber-speaking tribes driven out from the Mediterranean coastal strip by the Arabs. The Berbers created hilltop fortresses as a defense against attacks by the new occupiers of the region. In places as far apart as Gharyān in Libya and Matmâta in Tunisia, Berbers adapted to desert life in troglodite settlements, in which people dug out the rooms of their houses in the soft limestone or loess of the uplands. By the 1350s CE, transdesert trading stations grew up in the south of the Sahara; among them Tombouctou became one of the most important.

New World settlements

The Spanish conquest of the Americas in the 16th century CE resulted in the establishment of many colonial ports and administrative centers, many in deserts such as the cold Patagonian Desert of South America and the hot deserts of California. Urban forms were taken from Spain and were dominated by military and religious influences imported by the Spanish colonial authorities, particularly from Andalucía. In later centuries, the towns in the American deserts took on regional characteristics of their own, particularly those in North America, although Spanish influences are still apparent through the development of sites chosen by the Spanish and in the names of towns such as Los Angeles, Santa Fe, and Albuquerque.

GROWTH WITH WEALTH

Large cities have existed in many deserts for thousands of years. Many, such as Makkah and Al Qahira (Cairo), were trading or religious centers. However, largescale urbanization, particularly of Arabian and North American deserts, occurred only when mineral exploration showed the wealth of many desert regions and modern water management techniques made it possible to extract and transport enough water to satisfy the needs of large cities. Migration from rural areas to towns, particularly in developing countries, has also played an important role in the explosive growth of cities. Sometimes the local groundwater is used for irrigation, leaving insufficient for other uses. In Ar Riyāḍ (Riyadh) in Saudi Arabia desalinated water for domestic and municipal use is pumped 270 miles (450 kilometers) from desalination plants on the Gulf to the 1,700-feet (600-meter) elevation of the city.

▼ *Smoke from* the *Ābādān oil refinery in southwestern Iran fills the sky. Oil was first discovered near Abadan as early as 1908, and by 1913 the city was the oil-refining center of Persia (modern Iran). The city's proximity to large oil fields ensured it was the focus of much fighting during the Iran-Iraq War (1980–88).*

▶ *Opened in 1979,*
Kuwait Towers in Al
Kuwayt rise high above
the city. A symbol of
the city's vast oil wealth,
two of the towers hold
water, a less accessible,
but equally vital
commodity for the city.

Liquid gold

Oil, more than any other commodity, brought rapid and sustained urban growth in the deserts, first in North America and later in Arabia and the Gulf in the Middle East, and Saharan North Africa. Oil exploitation required new mining and service towns, such as Ābādān in Iran and ad Dammām in Saudi Arabia, which were located in the oil fields themselves. Oil brought great wealth to formerly poor desert economies, and an era of rapid and extensive town building began throughout the Arabian, Iranian, and North African deserts in the 1960s, exploding during the 1970s in response to the massive increase in oil revenues. Largescale construction occurred not just in the oil-producing states themselves. Countries such as Jordan and Egypt, which supplied oil transit facilities, labor, and political support, also underwent rapid urban expansion.

Provision of services for desert settlements is expensive and in the oil-producing areas can be supported only because large revenues are earned from oil exports. The population of Al Kuwayt (Kuwait City), for example, is reliant on oil for as much as 90 per cent of its income. A failure, or gradual fall, in oil revenues would make many of the urban settlements of the oil-exporting world entirely unsustainable.

85

The most spectacular development in the region has been that of Dubayy (Dubai). In the 1990s its rate of growth and range of activities increased. By 2005 its global role was reflected in its takeover of international transport and port management companies. The expansion of banking, property, airline, IT, bloodstock, and tourism activities established Dubayy as a center of global significance.

A developed economy

In the complex economy of the United States, settlements in semiarid regions have been used for a great variety of purposes. Much of the North American desert and the surrounding semi-desert was not attractive for farming during the westward expansion of the United States. By the 1950s, however, dams controled the flows of major rivers and modern irrigation supported rich orchard and arable estates, and made possible the growth of cities such as Las Vegas and Phoenix.

Rising standards of living after World War II made it possible for millions of people to move to life in the Sun Belt—in states such as Colorado, California, Texas, New Mexico, Arizona, and Nevada. The trend was led by older people seeking warmer places for their retirement, where they could pursue sports in reliable weather conditions. Tourism and recreation became an increasingly important industry in the Sun Belt. Industrial towns also grew up because the dry climate suited certain industries, and the sunshine is popular with the workforce. The rapid growth of Phoenix, Arizona, reflects these developments. Phoenix's water supply was originally ensured by the building of the Theodore Roosevelt Dam on the Salt River in 1911, but by the 1950s, mainly because of the introduction of air conditioning, the population rapidly grew, and the city's area increased from 17 square miles (44 square kilometers) to around 200 square miles (500 square kilometers) by the late 1980s. This expansion made necessary the construction of the Central Arizona Project, which diverts water from the Colorado River and began supplying Phoenix in 1986.

▲ **Despite the scarcity** *of water surrounding the desert gambling resort of Las Vegas, thanks to damming and pipeline projects, sufficient water has been found to ensure golf courses feature lush greens and numerous water hazards.*

▼ **Roosevelt Lake** and
its famous dam once
combined to create the
largest artificial lake in
the world. The lake was
intended to supply
Phoenix with all its water
requirements, but the
city's rapid growth in the
1960s and 1970s resulted
in additional water
having to be diverted
from the Colorado River.

This kind of growth has placed unsustainable pressures on the natural environment. In the Central Valley of California, and in many other places, shortages of water for urban use are reflected in periodic rationing of water supplies. The cost of providing water in desert areas is rising worldwide. There is competition for water between towns and the countryside; water is increasingly being bought by towns and the share of water available for farming decreases. Meanwhile, pumping of underground aquifers to supply urban needs has depleted fossil aquifers almost to extinction. Around the Great Sand Desert of Iran, for example, many villages, having pumped out their subsurface supplies, must now survive on low volumes of brackish water.

DESERT RESOURCES

Regions of many deserts are rich enough in resources to sustain the lives of large communities, although in the past this has only been in unusually favored locations, such as major river valleys. Until recent times, the most valuable resource for desert peoples was water. New technologies, however, have made it possible to exploit mineral deposits hidden beneath many of the world's deserts. The most obvious example is that of oil in the Arabian Peninsula, a resource so great that it has turned some of the world's poorest countries into economies with very high incomes. Absorbing these revenues has proved to be very challenging. Physical infrastructures have been transformed but it has proved to be very difficult to transform these economies into economically and socially sustainable political entities. Where opencast mining has been carried out, great areas of land have been spoiled; all forms of mining create large amounts of waste and the processing of ores can produce deadly toxins.

THE RICHES OF THE DESERT

Throughout history, deserts have been regarded as empty, inhospitable places. To all but an enterprising few, they have been barriers to movement and trade. People living in the desert have had to develop survival strategies based on the conservation of very scarce resources. In recent decades, however, the extraction of hydrocarbons and other minerals has brought about the transformation of some desert societies.

The traditionally used desert resources are vegetation and water. Most of these are renewable, including major rivers, some groundwater resources, and pasture. Some are nonrenewable, notably most deep groundwater resources.

Deserts have formed minor parts of the world's agricultural economy, but new technologies for water management have allowed some desert areas, such as southern California, to produce abundant fruit and vegetables. However, for most desert peoples, livestock rearing, or pastoralism, has long been the only viable economy. In the late 20th century, the need to feed rising populations has played a part in leading many desert states to adopt unsustainable agricultural policies. As a result, water and soil have been both diminished and degraded. In some regions, modern extraction and irrigation technologies have severely depleted groundwater or led to the salinization of the soil.

Non-renewable water resources have become increasingly important in desert regions. Most of these are waters accumulated over the last 100,000 years. Since the 1930s, the search for crude oil in the Middle East, Central Asia, and North Africa has led to the discovery of much of this water and its subsequent exploitation.

Energy and minerals

In economic terms, the most important resources of desert regions are crude oil and natural gas. Where oil came from is still somewhat of a mystery, but many geologists now believe it came from the breakdown of saltwater plankton and bacteria living in salty desert lakes and seas in the geological past. Some states with large crude oil deposits have become fabulously wealthy: Kuwait and the United Arab Emirates enjoy the highest gross national products per head of any countries in the world. Oil has also indirectly benefited both regional and global economies, giving employment to many millions of workers in oil-rich countries. At times, around 20 percent of Egypt's gross domestic product has been generated by remittances sent home by citizens working in the oil states.

Industrial activity is not extensive in desert economies. Until the 1980s, most crude oil was exported rather than processed near the source. The first oil crisis, in 1973, enabled oil-rich governments to invest in plant and equipment, and during the 1980s desert economies won an increasing share of oil-based energy and chemical production.

Deserts are also important repositories of non-renewable minerals. The Sahara is one example, containing important iron ore and phosphate deposits. The deserts of Iran are rich in minerals, including copper, those of North America and South America in copper and nitrates, and those of Australia in a wide range of mineral ores.

◀ *Elaborate irrigation systems allow a few citrus growers to wrest profits from the Anza-Borrego Desert, San Diego County, southern California. A wilderness of desert, chaparral, and mountains, much of the eastern two-thirds of San Diego County is unpopulated and unfarmed.*

The major renewable resources of desert regions is solar energy. To date, the only large-scale use of solar energy has been to heat water in homes. These systems have been widely adopted in Israel and Jordan, as well as in the conservation-conscious parts of the southwestern United States. Tapping the full potential of the Sun's energy requires more advanced technologies to convert the energy into usable forms.

The solar energy industry has been boosted by the four-fold increase in crude oil prices in 2005. The major energy companies involved in oil exploration and distribution have diversified into solar and other energies. Governments have also committed substantial funding and incentives to develop renewable solar energy installations. These arrays require very large areas, in which deserts are happily rich.

Desert economies are deficit economies

Renewable natural resources of the deserts are subject to degradation, while non-renewable ones are diminished by use. Neither is equal to the challenge of sustaining the current population. Consequently, food and other commodities must be imported. Although the extraction and exportation of crude oil and its derivatives are beneficial in the short term, they are based on the progressive depletion of national assets. Each year, desert economies are depleting natural resources, without establishing balancing value-adding activities to secure the livelihoods of succeeding generations. The move to industrialization that took place in the 1980s is one of the few strategies that might secure the future. Others include the investment of oil revenues in international capital markets and involvement in financial and banking services. In the past decade, the political leadership in Dubayy (Dubai) has mobilized entrepreneurship that has demonstrated that scarce environmental resources can be combined imaginatively with other capital. Capital derived from oil revenues, from financial services, and from tourism has been combined with the human capital of a very diversely skilled international immigrant population.

The Dubayy experiment contradicts any lingering beliefs that people might have that the environmental resource scarcity, such as is exemplified in deserts, determines low levels of economic activity.

▲ **Aerial view** of the ARCO-Solar photovoltaic power plant in the Mojave Desert, California, which supplies enough electricity to power 2,500 homes. One of the few renewable resources deserts do have to offer is sunlight. The development of a cheap method of mass-producing electricity directly from sunlight could transform the economies of many desert areas that lack substantial oil and gas deposits.

Livestock rearing is the main livelihood for many people living on desert margins. It is a very efficient way of using environments that cannot sustain agriculture, and if well-managed, can be very profitable. The risks are also great, the main one being drought, but there are also those of fluctuations in the price of animal products and animal diseases like rinderpest. Nomadic herding is very appropriate to deserts, given the unreliability and sporadic nature of desert margin rainfall, and the seasonality of their rainfall. In Sudan, the Kabbabish keep to the edge of the savanna in the dry season, clustered round the few reliable wells, but in the wet season they may be hundreds of miles north on the edge of the desert, making use of the protein-rich grasses that grow in what they call the *gizzu*, to feed their highly profitable camels. A nomadic lifestyle is also necessary to get stock to markets. The Darb el Arba'in (Forty Days Road) in the Sudan tells this story: it took Sudanese herders 40 days to get their camels to the great markets across the desert in Egypt.

▼ **Tuareg nomads** tend to their cattle by a well in the desert in Mali. Nomadic pastoralism does not convert easily into modern ranching. These cattle, for example, cannot forage for their own food in these desert conditions, and must be fed on scarce fodder that has been harvested elsewhere, requiring additional transportation.

Traditional strategies

Most livestock rearing is on the desert margins, but nomads may visit areas with very low rainfall after occasional rains, and some of them also move far south among agriculturalists in dry seasons or dry years. Few nomads or sedentary herders ever depended on their stock alone. There may have been seasons when they consumed very little but milk, but they

always also ate millet or some other grain. To buy grains, tea, and sugar, they traded their milk, meat, or animals with agri-culturalists on the desert's edge or in the oases. Alternatively, they sold their labor to harvest dates while in more modern times they do so for all sorts of industries, like construction. Many nomads also earned, and still earn, a living by taking goods or travelers across the desert. They plied many ancient routes like those across the Sahara to the Romans, across Arabia to places of pilgrimage like Makkah (Mecca), or along the Old Silk Road in central Asia. Today, many nomads indulge in smuggling people, drugs, and illicit goods of all sorts or take tourists into remote parts of the desert. To do this many have swapped their camels for lorries or four-wheel drives and have found that their survival and navigational skills are just as necessary with a vehicle as with a camel

Domesticated animals

The camel is the major livestock resource of the semiarid regions of northern Africa and Asia. There are two species—the Bactrian, two-humped camel of Central Asia and the dromedary (often also called a camel) of the drier parts of Asia and Africa. They are both hardy animals, able to with-stand heat and to go without drinking for long periods. In addition to providing meat, milk, wool, and leather, camels

▼ *Young goats* play on rock in the Negev Desert. Although goats (many of them from breeds adapted to very dry conditions), have an evil reputation among some older ecologists, they are very good at exploiting desert resources; they forage more efficiently than sheep, and by controlling plants that complete with sheep-forage, may, if carefully managed increase the productivity of sheep with no detriment to their own productivity.

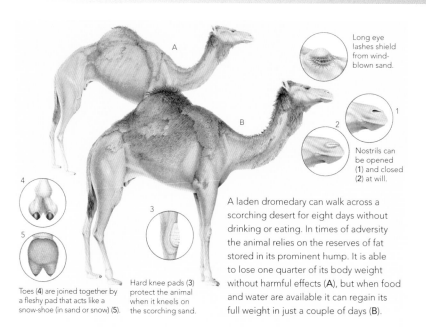

Long eye lashes shield from wind-blown sand.

Nostrils can be opened (1) and closed (2) at will.

Toes (4) are joined together by a fleshy pad that acts like a snow-shoe (in sand or snow) (5).

Hard knee pads (3) protect the animal when it kneels on the scorching sand.

A laden dromedary can walk across a scorching desert for eight days without drinking or eating. In times of adversity the animal relies on the reserves of fat stored in its prominent hump. It is able to lose one quarter of its body weight without harmful effects (A), but when food and water are available it can regain its full weight in just a couple of days (B).

have traditionally also been the major transport animal. Like the camel, the goat is a robust animal, well able to withstand the extreme environment and poor forage of the central desert tracts. Sheep are the major economic livestock, with their meat and other products always commanding higher prices than those from the goat. In the New World deserts, alpacas and llamas fulfill the same role as goats and camels (they also belong to the camel family). Cattle are generally not suited to desert conditions, although they are a feature of the agriculture of river valleys, where they are used for draft purposes, for transport, and for milk and meat. In some river valleys in the deserts, water buffalo are used for the same kind of uses.

Modern farming has deployed high technology to support livestock rearing in desert areas. Irrigated grain and alfalfa production in the Kufrah region of southeast Libya and intensive irrigation schemes around Ar Riyāḍ (Riyadh) have been used to support large populations of cattle and sheep. In terms of the depletion of natural resources (particularly of scarce groundwater), the cost of such projects has been immense. As a result, the experiment in southern Libya was abandoned by the end of the 1980s, although the Saudi Arabian schemes have been maintained.

TRADITIONAL FARMING

All of the world's great civilizations were founded beside the exogenous rivers that carry water to the desert. Their water ensured a reliable agricultural economy on which a civilized superstructure could be built. This was the case on the Eurphrates and Tigris (the Mesopotamian civilizations), Nile (the early Egyptian and Sudanese civilizations), and the Indus (the Harappan civilizations). All could depend on a reliable supply of water, fertile silt carried by the river, good alluvial soils and high inputs of sunlight. Irrigation enabled unprecedented levels of crop production. Many of the early systems of irrigation survive almost intact.

The system in the Nile Valley of Egypt and Sudan made use of the annual flood, which reached Egypt in the late summer. The waters also brought silt, which annually enriched the fields of the narrow Nile floodplain and the delta. After the annual flood had retreated, water had to be raised to the fields for dry-season crops. This was achieved by a variety of ingenious lifting devices, including the *shaduf*, a cantilevered, pivoting "seesaw" device, and the Archimedes' screw.

Elsewhere in the arid world, particularly in Persia, another form of ancient technology also ensured reliable agricultural production. The Persian wheel lifted groundwater from depths of up to 65 feet (20 meters), and was then used to lift

Qanats carry groundwater for irrigated areas (**1**) without evaporation. When a *qanat* is built, first a headwell (**2**) is sunk down to the water table (**3**). This well may be 330 ft (100 m) deep. A line of ventilation shafts is dug (**4**) and then an underground channel (**5**) is begun from the *qanat* mouth (**6**). Gravity moves water to the mouth where it is needed, and water can be drawn from the shafts (**7**).

water from channels up to the level of fields. The system has been adopted in many of the arid parts of northeast Africa to northern India. The precise origin of other invention of great hydraulic significant associated with Persia, the *qanat* (also known as the *falaj* in Oman and *foggara* in North Africa) is not known. It has been most extensively used in Persia (modern Iran), and examples of the technology have been observed in Algeria, Tunisia, Pakistan, China, Libya, Syria, Afghanistan, and even in Japan. These laboriously constructed, graded underground tunnels conveyed water sometimes tens of miles from distant groundwater sources to dry tracts that enjoyed good soil and other conditions favorable for agriculture.

Sustainability

Most of the ancient technologies, when compared to modern methods, were sustainable in terms of water use, largely because they were able to make use of only a small proportion of the water available to them. In the flood season water was diverted from the river at small weirs and simple canals, and their water-lifting devices were limited in their effectiveness by the energy available from animal or human power. Likewise the huge input of human energy in building *qanats* ensured that they were never able to tap all the available water in the alluvial fan.

The prosperous towns and villages of Persia that were once supplied by the sustainable subsurface *qanats*, and large oases in the Algerian Sahara that were once supplied by shallow wells have both been seriously affected by modern deep wells and mechanical pumps. These raise much more water than could ever have been supplied by the traditional systems, and in so doing have lowered the groundwater level to below that of the wells or *qanats*, rendering them redundant. Moreover, the rehabilitation of the ancient systems is impossible when either the physical or social infrastructure on which they depended has been damaged. Just as damaging to maintaining the old systems are social changes, such as emigration which removes the labor and the finance needed to maintain the tunnels or wells. Rehabilitation, however, has been possible in some of the Omani *qanats* and ancient South American irrigation systems. The open canals of the Patacancha Valley in Peru have been restored and are again providing water.

Rainfed farming

As paradoxical as it may sound, for thousands of years some desert peoples have relied on rain to grow crops in parts of arid regions where irrigation is not possible. One method,

which is very ancient and is widespread in Asia and Africa, is "runoff farming." In this system the water that runs off slopes is collected in fields in the valley bottoms. In the most sophisticated systems, slopes were cleared of gravel, so that runoff would be faster, and water was led down to the valley by a series of small channels. One particular example has been recreated at Avdat in the Negev Desert of Israel, and functions as it did (disproving theories that it had only been possible in antiquity because there had been more rainfall). The system is very labor intensive and somewhat risky, because it depends on sporadic rainfall. Similar systems from the Roman period have been found in Libya. In some countries, experiments with new techniques are resuscitating the runoff farming system

▲ Traditional methods *of bringing groundwater to the surface have benefited desert communities for thousands of years. Modern methods of extraction can deplete water resources in a matter of decades.*

Catch-crops

Even more surprising are fields that are sown only in wet years. In central Sudan, on the very edge of the real desert, sandy fields are sown with millet only in years when there has been good rain. In dry years the landscape appears like a desert, with no sign of cultivation. Sandy soils are particularly good for this purpose, because they rapidly absorb rain (there is virtually no runoff), and store it in the subsoil, from where it is unable to be evaporated because water cannot be drawn up by capillarity through the coarse pores in the surface layer of dry sand. Such crops are known as "catch-crops." In North Africa and southwestern Asia, similar systems raise barley and wheat. A rainfall of about 8 inches (200 millimeters) in any year is required to ensure a good crop of grain or straw (but of course the mean annual rainfall is much less).

The human and animal populations of arid areas have been expanding rapidly since the beginning of the 20th century, especially in the past 50 years. In the past, population levels were naturally regulated by periodic famines and even today some of the peoples living in the world's deserts endure extreme hardship. Natural resources augmented by traditional irrigation technology have not provided food security. The development of water resources by modern techniques of water management had been seen as a way to solve this problem.

For thousands of years, dams have been built in arid regions. The Marib Dam of Yemen and the structures built during the Roman period throughout the Middle East and North Africa are among the finest examples. These structures were often temporary and created few, if any, environmental problems. Since the beginning of the 20th century, however, large structures have been built throughout the dry areas of the world to control the supply of water. At first, these immense structures were built for agricultural purposes, but they were soon developed to provide hydroelectric power. In this way, ever greater volumes of water were diverted from their original courses, often resulting in the destruction of ecologically important floodplains and deltas.

▼ *A collapsed* section of the Marib Dam, Yemen. Work on the dam is believed to have started in about 1000 BCE and took 500 years to complete. The dam was regularly repaired and maintained until about 500 CE. The purpose of the dam was not to store water for long periods, but to divert the course of water in times of flash flooding. During the 4th century CE the dam's diverted water helped to irrigate 25,000 acres (10,000 hectares).

Other kinds of mismanagement affect the river valleys of the Old World deserts because the river basins are divided between more than one country; the Nile, the Tigris-Euphrates, and the Indus are particularly affected. These rivers are fed by water from upland Ethiopia, the East African Highlands, the mountains of Turkey and Iran, and the Himalayas. Because water loss through evaporation is lower at higher altitudes, dams sited in these upland regions would provide more economical storage than occurs from reservoirs deep in the arid deserts such as the High Dam at Aswân between Egypt and the Sudan. Such dams regulate the rivers and make more water available for economic purposes. At the same time they cause substantial water losses through evaporation, even at high altitudes, and change the ecology of the rivers by ending the natural annual flood cycle.

An irreplaceable resource

Water stored underground is safe from depletion by evaporation. Groundwater occurs naturally beneath vast tracts of the deserts of the world and such water is often of sufficient quality for human consumption and for irrigation. A high proportion of the groundwater of the Asian and African deserts is "fossil" water that has accumulated in wetter periods of the past 100,000 years. These ancient and generally finite groundwater resources have been severely depleted throughout the deserts of the world since the 1960s and 1970s. In the United States, pumping and water distribution technologies were developed and widely deployed to exploit groundwater in the southern states of Texas, Colorado, Arizona, and California. This has led to massive extractions of groundwater and to a rapid drop in water levels. The result was increased water costs, which have made a great deal of farming progressively less economically and ecologically viable.

Because deserts can bloom if water supplies are sufficient, engineers have, over the years, evolved ways of transporting water from basins in neighboring water-rich areas to desert regions. Vast new tracts were irrigated using unlined channels during the second half of the 19th century and the first half of the 20th century, enabling the increasing populations of desert countries such as Egypt, Iraq, India (including the present Pakistan), and Central Asia to be employed and fed.

These inter-basin transfers have been extremely important in terms of the volume of economic activity generated. Since the 1950s, water transfers between basins have been increasing in significance. In the United States, transfers of water from the Colorado Basin to southern California are crucial to this desert economy. However, arid northern

▲ **Largescale spray** *irrigation taking place on a farm in Arizona. Throughout the world the use of fossil groundwater for agriculture, particularly in the past 40 years, has transformed arid regions into valuable farmland. Losses of water because of evaporation are high, however, and this resource is being seriously depleted.*

Mexico has been adversely affected by these water exports from the Colorado Basin because they reduce flow in the Colorado river. In turn, Mexico itself has had plans to engineer transfers of water from it well-watered western and southern mountains to the arid north of the country. The flow of the Rio Grande has been reduced by a combination of human intervention and periods of lower than average rains. Mexico was for many years unable to deliver the water, as stipulated in the US-Mexico transboundary agreement.

The dangers of such huge water transfers have become apparent in the former Soviet Union. Here, the agricultural development of the arid south was to be based on the transfer of water from the rivers of the humid north or mountainous east. Only part of the scheme has been completed; the consequences for the Aral Sea have been disastrous, and the livelihoods of local people and the local ecology have been ruined.

RESHAPING THE LAND

New technology has made it possible to prepare land for cultivation more quickly than in the past, and to cultivate more thoroughly and more often. At the same time, water technologies have enabled people to lift and move massive quantities of water over great distances, as well as to distribute it to vast irrigated tracts. The ability to manage soil and water resources in these ways has had many very powerful impacts on the surface and subsurface of the world's deserts.

The capacity to disturb the land surface and to remove the natural protective shrub and herb cover has led to the degradation of extensive areas of the world's deserts. The Middle East and North Africa have many tracts of dry land that have been irreversibly damaged by attempts to undertake cultivation far beyond that which could be sustained by existing levels of rainfall. Extensive parts of Iraq, Syria, and Jordan have been seriously degraded. In Libya, Algeria, and northwest Egypt, marginal land has had its agricultural and ecological potential destroyed through soil erosion caused by such attempts at cultivation.

Greening the deserts

The increased use of water that has been made possible by modern techniques can improve agricultural production, but rarely increases economic productivity when costs and investment are taken into consideration.

▼ *A fountain* in the shape of a coffee pot illustrates the significance of water in desert cities such as Abū Ẓāby (Abu Dhabi). The treelined boulevards and stretches of neatly manicured lawns indicate how "green" many desert cities aspire to be.

The greening of desert areas for both irrigated farming and the amenity of gardens and trees in the countryside and the city is generally welcomed. The desert countries of the Gulf have invested heavily on improving the appearance of whole cities and of long stretches of roads. Abū Ẓāby (Abu Dhabi), for example, has achieved such a remarkable level of "greening" in its major urban centres that they can now almost be regarded as garden cities.

The use of high volumes of water can at the same time have a number of serious negative consequences. All water contains some salts and so can cause salinization of soil, especially in desert areas where evaporation is high. Such salinization is not a new phenomenon. Ancient irrigation schemes faced similar problems, but the pace of deterioration is quicker now because modern water management techniques have made possible interventions on an unprecedented scale.

Poor water management also leads to poorer groundwater quality. Water that passes through a layer of soil tends to accumulate salts, and can reach high concentrations. Salinized water that moves down to the water table pollutes the groundwater resource and restricts its further use in agriculture.

▲ **Imperial Valley** in southern California relies solely on the Colorado River, via the All American Canal, for its water requirements. The border between the United States and Mexico is clearly defined by a break in the degree of irrigation.

Careful management

Despite all these problems, modern technology can also provide very important benefits for the efficient use of scarce water. Indeed, the successful management of the world's deserts is, to a considerable extent, a matter of the effective management of technology. Metering systems can assist farmers and project managers to regulate the use of water. Such regulation can be automated. In one kind of system, sensors are distributed through an irrigated area and pass information back to a computer that controls irrigation; the computer ensures the optimum availability of water to crops while at the same time minimizing its use. At the level of a small farm, modern water distribution system known as "trickle" or "drip" systems deliver water in carefully controlled amounts; such systems can increase the efficiency of water use by more than 100 percent for crops that can be grown in rows and for tree crops.

The extent to which modern technology has positive or negative effects on the surface and the subsurface depends on the manner in which it is used. Technology can be environmentally appropriate when properly managed. When it is used carelessly, its full destructive capacity to disturb and irreversibly damage soil and groundwater is brought to bear. Sound water technology must be the basis of the future utilization of the world's deserts. It will, therefore, be very important to develop effective institutions at all levels—from national governments to individual farms—to deploy and regulate the use of these powerful technologies.

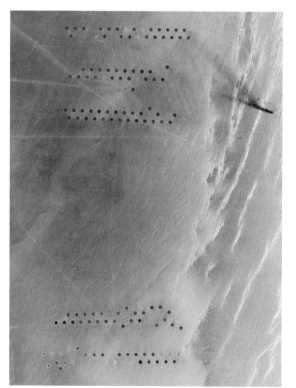

◀ *A picture generated by an imaging satellite showing irrigated fields near the al Kufrah Oasis in Libya. The distinctive circular shapes produced by center-pivot irrigation equipment are clearly visible. Variations in the apparent color of the fields indicate crops at different stages of growth. The smoke on the right is gas burnoff from an oil well.*

Modern drilling, pumping and distribution systems have made it possible to lift groundwater in remote desert areas from depths as great as 1,600 feet (500 meters). Once out of the ground, the water can be applied over enormous areas according to schedules that meet the irrigation requirements of a wide range of crops.

The main technology to have developed relatively recently for utilizing groundwater in agriculture is the center-pivot structure. Water is conveyed under pressure from the central source by means of an electric pump. It then flows along a moving gantry, which circles around the source distributing the water over the crops. The speed at which the equipment circles is regulated as necessary to determine the frequency of application of the water.

The result of the center-pivot system is a dramatic circle of vegetation in a barren sea of sand. A major advantage of the system is that it can be operated on quite uneven land, which means that the high costs of land leveling can be avoided. On the other hand, it has been found in the United States—where center-pivot equipment is widely used for supplementary irrigation in the dry southwest and in some of the arid mountain states—that better germination and growing conditions occur when preparatory leveling had been carried out. The main problem is that on irregular surfaces water tends to accumulate in the hollows and drain from higher parts, leading to uneven access to water and variations in crop development.

Theory into practice

In 1971, Libyan officials were advised that the high-quality groundwater of the Kufrah Basin would enable the production of wheat to help the country become self-sufficient in this staple crop. Unfortunately, the wheat project was not successful and by the mid-1970s it was decided that a 25,000-acre (10,000-hectare) livestock scheme, based on the production of alfalfa, would be a preferable strategy. Difficulties arose, however, not because of low availability of water or inadequacies in the soil, but through the harmful effects of hot dry winds on plants and livestock, and ultimately because the health of the sheep flocks could not be adequately maintained.

Also in Libya, an even larger scheme covering some 125,000 acres (50,000 hectares) was attempted in the Sarir Basin, drawing on another resource of ancient groundwater. Again, the project encountered problems, not the least of them being social. The organizational and technical difficulties led the Libyan government to switch to a strategy of piping water from the southern aquifers to the coast, which is where the users of the water preferred to live.

The most extensive deployment of the center-pivot system outside the United States has been accomplished in Saudi Arabia. A wish to achieve food self-sufficiency, combined with seeming unlimited supplies of capital from oil revenues, brought about a government-led policy to utilize the groundwater of the Ar Riyāḍ (Riyadh) region. Many hundreds of thousands of hectares were developed for irrigated farming. By 1990, Saudi Arabia was raising a significant proportion of the country's animal feed requirements as well as becoming, rather surprisingly, an exporter of wheat and a number of other agricultural products.

The sustainability of the desert irrigation projects around Riyadh is, however, very much in doubt. They are not economically secure because the output is only achieved at many times the world price for the commodities produced. Moreover, the groundwater supply, which is only partially renewed each year, is being rapidly depleted.

A free commodity

The center-pivot systems, although relatively water-efficient compared to other methods of irrigation, are not ideal in terms of water conservation compared with various drip systems. The latter, however, can only be used with a narrow range of trees and crops. As a result, drip systems are not popular, especially where the dangerous perception prevails that water is free.

Governments throughout the arid world have difficulty managing a resource that has been traditionally viewed as free, albeit precious in terms of availability. Attitudes are difficult to change, especially once it seemed that water has become more abundant. Most government bodies are loath to argue for ecologically and economically sound water resource allocation in the face of élite organizations and professional interests that argue for the development of water for farming in the misguided belief that it will create long-term wealth and self-sufficiency.

Water pipelines

Water scarcity has been addressed by pipelines and other water-transfer technologies. The earliest scheme was the pipeline built in the early 20th century to bring water from the Owens River in eastern California to the rapidly developing and very thirsty population of Los Angeles. Other phases of the California State Water Project have brought water from the north and from the Colorado River. The

▲ *A water pipeline runs through Owens Valley in California. The valley was the setting for a bitter confrontation over water rights between valley farmers and residents and the city of Los Angeles. So much water was diverted to the city that the valley's main water source, Owens Lake, is now completely dry.*

Israeli state has also built a water carrier to convey freshwater from Lake Tiberias/Kinneret. The original intent was to green the Negev Desert, but the water has proved to be more valuable for municipal water supplies. Libya's Great Manmade River—begun in 1980, with the final phase due for completion in 2008—is a desert phenomenon conveying water in pipes 13 feet (4 meters) in diameter across thousands of miles of desert to the arid and semiarid coastal tracts at the Mediterranean.

OIL AND GAS

The world's oil industry dates from 1859, when Colonel Edwin Drake began processing oil from shallow seepages in Pennsylvania, in the United States. The industry grew rapidly as American oil companies sought new, easily exploitable reserves. In particular, their search took them to the desert areas of the west and southwest of North America, and major discoveries were made in the arid regions of Texas and California. The desert areas of Mexico were also explored and developed for petroleum at an early date. Deserts were easy for the oil companies to explore and develop. The absence of vegetation made geological surveying straightforward and there was little existing industry or agriculture to compete with oil exploitation.

The process of exploration began seriously in the early 1900s when the world's largest resources were discovered beneath the deserts of the Middle East and North Africa. In 1908, oil was discovered at Mesjed-e Sulaiman on the fringes of the Khuzestan Desert in Iran by a company that eventually became British Petroleum. Elsewhere in the Persian Gulf region, exploration was spurred on by the finds in Iran. Oil was soon found in Iraq, Saudi Arabia, Kuwait, and Bahrain, although development was delayed by the advent of World War II. At the same time, the Sahara, the Australian, and South American deserts of were all explored.

Oil was later discovered in the Libyan Desert as far south as the Calanscio and Marzūq Sand Seas, in Algeria at Hassi Massoud and in the cold deserts of Alaska and Siberia. But the Iranian, Arabian, and Iraqi deserts remained the most concentrated areas of oil and natural gas reserves. By 1991,

◄ *Oil exploration* in *the vast Libyan oil fields is on the increase since the lifting of US sanctions. The desert is a difficult place in which to work, however. Before any drilling can commence, a stable surface must be created amid the shifting sands. Throughout the lifetime of the rig, windblown sand is a machinery-clogging nuisance.*

the Middle East was estimated to have not less than 66 percent of all world crude oil and 30 percent of natural gas reserves. Oil production in this area was 26 percent of the world total. In North Africa, Egypt, Algeria, and Libya accounted for almost 6 percent of world oil output.

The history of the oil industry in the deserts is remarkably short. But the future of the industry may be equally short. Ratios of reserves to production rates indicate that many oil fields will soon reach the end of their useful lives—in about 10 years in the United States, 20 years in Oman, Qatar and Bahrain, and less than 50 years in many other areas. However, reserves in Saudi Arabia, Iran, Iraq, and Kuwait are so large that they may last much longer than this.

The short life of the oil industry contrasts sharply with its enormous ecological and human impact. The oil and natural gas industries have helped to bring rapid and sophisticated human development to poor areas. Generally, the oil industry has brought urban growth and welfare improvements to simple herding, gathering, and hunting economies.

A price to pay

The industry, however, has also abused deserts. For many years, natural gas, a by-product of oil, was simply burned off as a waste product, an action that generates atmospheric pollution. In the North American oil fields, thousands of acres of land are exploited by surface pumps and the surface is scarred with spoil. The low value of deserts leads to the use of unsuitable or dangerous technologies for storage and pipeline construction, while local flora and fauna are disregarded. Only in the United States has any form of conservation been attempted. The worst pollution occurs with disasters. In Kuwait, when Iraqi troops destroyed equipment, including wellheads, in oil fields during the 1990–91 Gulf War, millions of barrels of oil were spilled onto the land and into the waters of the Persian Gulf.

Perhaps equally harmful have been the activities of governments with oil revenues to spend. Belief in the need to stimulate "development" led to rapid growth of agricultural and industrial projects and their associated towns and infrastructures—all paid for by oil. In many oil-exporting countries, notably Saudi Arabia, huge petrochemical industries have been set up, bringing unforeseen problems to the desert, particularly the disposal of industrial waste. The natural resources in most desert states are unable to support sustained heavy industrial development and there is a real chance that for all the longterm negative environmental and ecological impact of modernization, the human benefits will be only shortlived.

MINING AND MINERALS

Most of the industry in deserts is based on extracting hydrocarbons and minerals. Apart from a small number of enterprises, such as tourism and moviemaking, that can gain some advantage from the climate, deserts offer few other positive attractions to industrialization.

Land is cheap in deserts, so largescale mineral extraction can be undertaken using huge areas for mining, marshalling and depositing ores and spoil. Exploration and survey work can be readily carried out in desert regions where the soil is thin and vegetation sparse. Until recently the visual pollution arising from these activities carried little stigma. Pollution of the atmosphere, the land and water supplies has been widespread and with few exceptions extractive industries in deserts have been exploitative and temporary.

The largest single extractive industry in deserts is for building materials. Most activities are small in scale, producing materials such as road stone, lime, chalk, gypsum, and building sand. This industry generally serves local markets because transportation costs of low-grade minerals are high in relation to the minerals' value.

Diamond mining in Namibia

Namibia's richest areas for diamonds are on the Diamond Coast, where the Namib Desert meets the Atlantic Ocean. The diamonds were formed in what is now South Africa, and were washed to the delta of the Orange River. From here coastal currents carried them north and deposited them on beaches along with other sediments. The beaches were buried as sedimentation continued.

Modern extraction methods involve huge open-cast pits. Massive earthen walls are built to hold back the sea, and excavation takes place to the level of the bedrock, as much as 66 feet (20 meters) below sea-level. The diamond mines leave mountains of discarded spoil, and when abandoned the workings flood with seawater to leave a huge checkered pattern along the coast.

Minerals of the desert

Much of the other mining that takes place in deserts is not directly related to the desert itself but to what lies under it. Some minerals are, however, related to the conditions prevailing in some deserts. The world's biggest deposits of phosphates, for example, are found in desert environments—particularly the Sahara and Jordanian deserts—and these are traded internationally on a large scale.

One of the world's hottest desert areas, the Dead Sea, is the center of two large potash industries, one In Israel and

▶ *A vast diamond-mining operation underway in Namibia. Diamond mining first began in Namibia as early as the first decade or two of the 20th century. Modern large-scale mining operations can cause a number of environmental problems.*

the other, just across the border, in Jordan. Both extract potash from the salty water on the shores of the Dead Sea, where falling water levels in the early 20th century caused concern to both parties. The potash is used in domestic industries and is exported, mainly as fertilizer.

In the Western Desert of Iraq, at sites such as Al-Qa'im, phosphates and natural sulfur are exploited for the chemical and petrochemical industries. Elsewhere, sulfur is produced as a byproduct of crude oil. Other minerals, including common salt, are mined in many deserts and provide the natural resource for local chemical industries.

Metals and precious stones

Largescale reserves of metallic ores are found in many deserts, some of which are important to world trade. Most copper, for example, comes from the fringes of the Atacama in South America and from Sar Cheshmeh in the high salt deserts of the Iranian Zagros Mountains. Considerable reserves of iron ore exist in the Sahara in Mauritania and southwestern Algeria, and in the Dasht-e Kavir Desert in Iran. Gold, silver, and precious stones are commonly associated with the mines in Australia, as well as in the Kalahari and North American deserts. Since the start of the nuclear age, uranium mining has become increasingly important. Some desert regions of Australia, the United States, and Namibia hold large reserves of uranium ore.

VISITING DESERTS

Deserts have many attractions: dependable sunshine, space, beauty, history (extremely old and not so old), moving dunes, singing sands, vast salt lakes, geology laid bare, amazingly well-adapted plant and animal species, extraordinarily far-traveling birds, exotic cultures, cheap accommodation and so on. But, before rushing to see these wonders, it is worth remembering their flip sides: the weather may be unbearably hot and dusty, even dangerous, if one meets the rare storm or gets lost. The weather may even be cold and wet in places like North Africa; the huge spaces can be oppressively empty or repetitive, and may also be dangerous to travel across unless one is sure of location, vehicle, and driving skill. Great beauties may either not be to one's taste or to many other people's tastes; the historical relics, curiosities, and wildlife are either a one-time wonder, only for the connoisseur or are also not for those who want space (particularly the tunnels into the pyramids); to say nothing about accommodation. In some minds, of course, the beautiful (the desert sky at night) and the awful (a scorpion in the sleeping bag) are complementary: real pleasure is bought with real discomfort.

THE FIRST DESERT TOURISTS

The double face of the desert has a long history in tourist literature. It was Napoleon who kick-started modern desert tourism. When he landed in Egypt in 1798, he brought not only an army of musketeers, but also another of antiquarians who began to discover the long history that we now know. Napoleon's battlefields (on the most critical of which he lost) were in a long line belonging to European desert wars, and still attract their share of tourists. Napoleon's discoveries were used to promote the desert as an adventurous extension to the Grand Tour. Celebrated writers like Kinglake (Palestine and Egypt in 1834), Flaubert (Egypt in 1850 and Tunisia 1858), and Mark Twain (1867) followed the extended tour, or parts of it, and stimulated the debate about the desert's two-facedness. Flaubert's joke, in which he surreptitiously dropped and then pretended to find the card of a French polisher from Rouen at the top of the Great Pyramid, anticipated generations of jokes about the two facets. Mark Twain, as a professional sceptic, made many more. Some of the early jokes are not so funny today: modern visitors to the pyramids are appalled to see large, deeply carved copperplate graffiti inscribed by 19th-century tourists (or more likely by masons they employed). Defacing ancient monuments was the prerogative of the privileged in those days.

▼ *The pyramids at Giza* have been a source of fascination for European visitors since the mid-19th century. The Great Pyramid itself was the tallest building on Earth for 43 centuries.

The "Eastern" tour

The "Near East," especially its deserts, is, as ever, the nearest place to Europe where tourists can find the authentic cultural and environmental exotic. The Egyptian ruins (and others as at Petra) have always been the biggest attractions, but a century and half ago tours were striking out to real desert phenomena, like the singing sands in Sinai (dubbed the "Mountain of the Bell" by tour guides of the time). Baedeker's first guide to Palestine and Syria was published in 1876; his first guide to Egypt in 1878.

The deserts of the American southwest became accessible to tourism after the building of the Southern Pacific Railroad transcontinental connection in the 1880s. Baedeker's guides to America and Mexico date from 1893. The Grand Canyon railway was opened in 1910, while the Grand Canyon itself became a National Park as early as 1919. The claim, often made, that the historical relics of the American deserts were puny when compared with those in the Near East, is no longer valid. Archaeologists have found a very rich history of settlement in the Southwest, not as old as in Egypt perhaps, but every bit as intriguing, especially in what it tells about living in the desert.

In this long history, tastes and judgements have changed many times and will undoubtedly change again. Stephen Pyne's history of the Grand Canyon teases out some strands from a rich tapestry: Spanish explorers were quite indifferent to the canyon; early American homesteaders were repulsed by its infertility; when European and North American taste discovered mountains, it was still unable to comprehend this negative mountain; but after the one-armed John Wesley Powell discovered something about the canyon's amazing geological history, there was a surge of interest that drew in the painters retrospectively assigned to the "American sublime;" and for a brief moment science and aesthetics met. President Theodore Roosevelt added a new aesthetic judgement when he gave a speech at the canyon in 1903: "Leave it as it is. You cannot improve on it. The ages have been at work on it, and man can only mar it." His successors, incidentally, paid little heed: nearly all the water in the Colorado is now used; its water is more saline than is allowed by international agreement, and most of its sediment is trapped behind several huge dams, where it is rapidly silting up the immense reservoirs.

The romantic desert

A fuller history of desert tastes would trace the roots of Roosevelt's speech. One is the tradition of the Christian "desert fathers," who sought God in desert wilderness. The most famous, St. Anthony, founded one of the monasteries that are now considerable tourist attractions in the Eastern desert of Egypt. A second ancestral idea dates back at least to the 14th-century Arab sociologist Ibn Khaldun who believed the desert to be the home of simple, uncorrupted, pure souls, a theme revived by Edward Gibbon and Charles Doughty (and Hollywood). A third tradition saw the desert as the epitome of romantic decay, as in Shelley's "Ozymandias" (1817) and a genre in 19th-century French romantic art. A fourth in

115

this ideological family was the desert as an example of environmental misuse (not at all romantic), as seen in the books of Paul Sears and Walter Lowdermilk, which held up the Middle-Eastern deserts as lessons on how not to manage the environment of the United States.

This fuller aesthetic history of deserts would also look at Roosevelt's descendants. It would find, first, that the old themes appeared in many new guises: the desert as T.E. Lawrence's war against himself and the British establishment; the desert of Rudolph Valentino, the cinematic Bedouin lover; the searing desert of British soldiers in *Ice Cold in Alex*; the Australian desert as inspiration for *Songlines* (Bruce Chatwin); as masculine Marlboro Country; as very female in Georgia O'Keeffe's paintings; and so on.

▲ **Deserts** are rapidly becoming areas for a variety of recreations. Dune-buggy drivers support the development of some desert regions to allow for services.

Technology vs technique

As an aesthetic history approached the present, it would cover two newer traditions. These were differentiated in Joseph Sax's book *Mountains without Handrails*. The first is the aesthetic of wilderness-seekers who want pure wilderness unsullied by people. They are the inheritors of Roosevelt's commandment: "Leave it as it is." They see themselves as approaching the wilderness with technique, rather than technology. They may tolerate a well-maintained Jeep, Land Rover, or motorcycle, if only because it is the most feasible way to approach the desert (without resorting to the camel). But they would insist that such a vehicle was to be driven by someone with the navigational and mechanical skills needed to travel far from the reach of most rescue services, and they insist on being in only small groups of intruders. They abhor the mass intrusions of the second group, which comprises those who regard the desert as a challenge to technology and who generally arrive in large groups. These are the sand-buggyers, four-wheel-drive and motorcycle club enthusiasts. Eight hundred thousand of them in a year, and as many as 80,000 of them on a single weekend may be found buggying on the Algodones Dunes in California. Others are to be found on the dunes of the United Arab Emirates and other rich deserts. To these people, intrusions into the desert (like food and drink stalls, and so on) are welcome. What they, in turn, abhor is the regulations imposed on them by the wilderness-seekers. The desert is not the only place to find the clash between these two strands of tourist (many lakes and forests suffer from similar issues), but the clash is much more obvious in the great open vistas of most deserts.

Today's desert tourists, consciously or unconsciously, carry all this baggage with them as they scan brochures and then try to make sense of the desert they choose. The travel literature panders to their preconceptions, but may anger them in retrospect. If they visit the sites that inspired the desert aesthetics of the past, they may find some of what they expect, especially if they take a slow pace, and choose dates and places with care. But yesterday's deserts are likely to disappoint innocents who think they are going to see anything like they saw in the classic films such as *Lawrence of Arabia* or *Death on the Nile*. There was a 161 percent increase in tourism to Egypt in 2005, the legacy, perhaps, of Napoleon, Flaubert, and Agatha Christie. Five million tourists now visit Tunisia each year (where much of *The English Patient* was shot), and four million of them reach Morocco (background to the classic desert novel by Paul Bowles, *The Sheltering Sky*, and the subsequent film). In each country the number of desert-visitors has been growing faster than the number who go to the coast. The tourist will find the Grand Canyon similarly burdened, although only on its North and South Rims, because descent to its depths is strictly controlled.

▼ **The obverse** to the high-octane recreational desert is the desert as unspoilt wilderness and place of wonder. This romantic view of deserts is still very much alive, and is fed by tourist operators keen to portray the desert as mysterious and exotic to would-be desert wanderers.

117

In some middle ground between familiar deserts and the more recently opened up deserts, are places like Iran, Rajasthan in India, and central Asia. These were well known to 19th-century readers, but too distant to attract many 19th-century tourists. In them the tourist can see exquisite and venerable ancient monuments, and the rich cultures that created them.

Today's tourists can also travel to places that, among Europeans and North Americans at least, were seen only by explorers a century ago. They no longer rely on steamships and trains (although some still choose them). Cheap airfares have opened up almost all of the deserts within reach of an airport. Four-wheel drive vehicles have prised open the once remote places beyond. Air conditioning has far surpassed punka wallahs and electric fans (and even the Maharaja of Jodhpur's system of pumping air through wet muslin). But even in some of these deserts, there are crowds of tourists. In 2003 some 400,000 people visited Uluru in the Australian desert. Baja California in Mexico is teeming.

A sustainable future

The more fastidious tourist will discover desecration far worse than graffiti. Vehicle tracks across many deserts are readily visible on Google Earth, even when tarmac roads are not. In places, as in Oman, there is meticulous collection of trash, but in many more, trash is very visible in huge peripheral areas of towns and along roads. New buildings, few of

▼ *Despite* its relative isolation in the Northern Territory, Uluru (Ayers Rock) is a prime destination for tourists, who are now served by a number of hotels, restaurants, tourist operators, and Aborignal guides.

▲ **A desire** by the developed global community to reduce carbon dioxide emissions has seen deserts becoming home to a variety of sustainable energy projects, such as this tiny wind-farm in the Sonoran Desert in California. But projects such as this are far from free of voiciferous criticism.

them well designed or well built, disfigure once idyllic coves, as in Sharm El Sheikh in southern Sinai. In the deserts of North America, retirement centers like Palm Springs and gambling centers like Las Vegas sprawl over enormous areas, within which there is a determined effort to blot out the desert with huge amounts of imported water on golf courses and suburban gardens. The sustainability of these cities, especially in terms of their water use, is very dubious. In many deserts there are huge military and space installations. Woomera in Australia is set in a security zone that covers 50,000 square miles (127,000 square kilometers). In the Sonoran Desert in California there are now some huge wind farms. There are 5,000 wind turbines in the Tehachapi Pass alone.

Preserving the past
More worrying, not only for later generations of tourists, but also for archaeologists, is damage to the desert's history. Ancient monuments (particularly if they are not well guarded, as many are not) are still defaced and stolen from. Some of the groups who now reach the Tassili scarplands in the central Sahara, which have very impressive cave and rock art, chip it off and take it home. Flints at the sites of Paleolithic and Neolithic "factories" across the Sahara are readymade souvenirs, and end up as such. Some are collected by local entrepreneurs and sold to tourists. This kind of vandalism is not confined to tourists. Oil men, of various sorts, have been stationed in remote desert camps for decades. For weekend recreation they collect artwork and artefacts, which they may accumulate in specially created exhibition boxes; but they very seldom take the care that an archaeologist would in noting the position and stratum from where the artefacts were collected. Little national legislation is in place to regulate these pressures, and even where there is, it is difficult to enforce. Some oil companies now have environmentally principled and heritage-sensitive guidelines. But new companies do not have these policies, and anyway much of the damage has already been done.

Of even greater concern, this time to conservationists as well as to tourists, is the effects of hunting. Hunting, even to extinction (locally and even globally) is not new to deserts. It probably eliminated the post-glacial megafauna of North America. North Africa and southwest Asia lost most of their large mammals to hunters in Roman times. In the 19th century Przewalski's horse was hunted to extinction (in the wild) in central Asia, and many other species were reduced to very small numbers. Hunting continues, even with populations so near to extinction. Large convoys of airconditioned caravans follow hunters across the deserts of Arabia, Sudan, and Kazakhstan. Remaining populations of gazelle, oryx, addax, Arabian Tahr, and Barbary sheep are on the brink of extinction. Game bird populations are declining fast, particularly of the Houbara bustard, the choice for hunters with falcons in Arabia and Kazakhstan.

Fortunately the deserts are vast. Only tiny areas of them are occupied by hotel complexes, golf courses, wind farms or space centers. If one's taste is space and little else, deserts have much to offer. There are vast bleak, almost featureless spaces in the Sahara: plains covered with small pebbles and with only very occasional vegetation in a few hollows. One can drive for days across the Calanscio Serir in Libya, the Tademaït in central Algeria, and the Tanezrouft in the south, the western Ténéré in northeastern Niger, or the Selima sand sheet in northern Sudan and southwestern Egypt. The Paris-Dakar rally, every year it seems, loses at least one vehicle in the Tanezrouft. There are more huge empty quarters in the northwestern Chinese Gobi.

Desert landscapes

There are huge fields of dunes (covering many hundreds of thousands of square miles), in which the specialist may be able to distinguish different kinds of dune, but the casual visitor may see seemingly endless repetition of forms and there are salt lakes that are almost as enormous. These landscapes are acquired tastes and visiting them still requires good guides, vehicles, and safety provision. Satellite navigation, satellite phones, and helicopter rescue services may have made them much safer places, but they are still dangerous.

Most tourists will want to visit landscapes with more relief or more variety, and there are many of these as well: the mountains and scarplands in the central Sahara; Uluru in central Australia; the wall of volcanoes in northern Chile; and the Grand Canyon and its attendant wonders in Arizona, Utah, and Nevada. For the coastal enthusiast, there are great

▶ US troops visit villages in the Ghrac Valley near Gardez, Afghanistan. Afghanistan was once a popular tourist destination, offering breathtaking scenery, important flora and fauna, and a rich cultural heritage. Tourism halted during the Russian invasion, Taliban rule, and the US and allied invasion, but there are now cautious attempts to revitalize the industry.

sights in the beaches and reefs of the Red Sea and in the Sea of Cortes (the Gulf of California). The Omani mountains, with their restored mud forts and amazing geology also have a high place on this list.

Desert conflicts

Security is a real issue both for the tourists themselves and for the tourist industry. The list of desert destinations that are safe (or relatively so) from banditry or military operations changes quite quickly. Sudan, Iran, Algeria, Libya, Syria and, of course Iraq and Afghanistan, open to tourism in the 1960s and even 1970s, have all been considered too dangerous for tourists in the last 30 years. Some still are, although there is slow growth of tourism in Iran and Algeria. The tourist industry in Chad and Niger was throttled in the 1980s and early 1990s by civil war. Chaddian tourism was under threat from unrest in early 2006. Yet deserts that were once off limits to the ordinary tourist have opened up in the last two decades: in Central Asia, Mongolia, and western China. These deserts are following in the footsteps of the older tourist destinations. Tourism contributed six percent to Tunisian GDP in 1999 and employed more than 300,000 people. Big sectors of the economy like this are only sustainable in politically secure and economically advanced environments. The tourist industry quails at hints of insecurity. Terrorism is a real, if rather random threat in Asian and North African deserts. Nor do

terrorists have to operate in deserts themselves to affect their tourist industry. After 9/11 tourist numbers fell drastically across the world.

In the medium term there are other major threats to desert tourist economies and businesses and, of course, to the opportunities open to tourists. A major one is the rising price of energy. When even Baedeker's successors (Lonely Planet and the Rough Guides), begin to warn their users to save energy, and when taxes on aircraft fuel are widely talked of, desert destinations, particularly the more distant ones should begin to worry.

Responsible practice

Ecotourism and community-based conservation are responses to some of these concerns about the environment. Ecotourism is low-impact tourism, which should not come up against issues of energy costs and competition for water; community-based conservation is a means of allowing more than a modest amount of income from tourists to reach disadvantaged people, for harnessing local knowledge and mitigating impacts like overgrazing.

But, it seems, the entrepreneurs developing ecotourism have not developed systems of self-regulation. Some tours that advertise themselves as ecotourism are palpably damaging to the environment and there are schemes that pay lipservice to community involvement, but still impose the will of central government or of entrepreneurs keen on profit. Community conservation is particularly difficult to manage, because there is always a conflict between the wish to profit and the requirement to conserve. More carefully defined, monitored, and marketed, ecotourism and community conservation have the potential to enhance nature conservation, and to contribute to local incomes.

▼ **Jet-skiers** prepare for a ride near the Burj Al Arab hotel. The Burj Al Arab is just one of many luxury hotels that have been built recently in Dubayy (Dubai), United Arab Emirates. As well as guaranteeing hot sunshine, dry weather, excellent sporting and shopping facilities, Dubayy can also supply a real desert experience.

North Africa and the Middle East

The Arabic language and culture may unite this region, but it includes tourist destinations with very different characteristics. At one end of the spectrum, Dubayy (Dubai) claims to be the world's fastest-growing tourist destination; 100,000 British people have bought homes there and it is aiming at 15 million tourist visits a year. In this hyperarid country with a punishing summer climate, new islands are being constructed offshore to accommodate luxury villas. Dubai already has some of the most luxurious hotels in the world, if not the single most luxurious. It annually hosts lavish international sporting competitions in horse racing, grandprix motor racing, cricket, tennis, golf, and rugby. A Disneyland complex and a wide range of other recreational and shopping facilities are planned. At the same time, Dubayy and its neighbors in the United Arab Emirates offer real desert experiences, such as four-wheel drive treks though lovely red dunes. Dubayy tops a tourist league that includes the other Emirates and Oman (which offers a bigger variety of authentic desert experiences).

Egypt is a special case: it has the unique ancient monuments and spectacularly well-stocked museums, but also fantastic desert scenery in the Eastern Desert and Sinai, and excellent beaches and reefs. Israel is also unique. Eilat on the Gulf of Aqaba has glorious desert scenery, good facilities and excellent reefs, but the area is small. However, the desert experience in Israel can be combined with visits to other, non-desert sites of world renown (in both Israel and Palestine).

The Maghreb countries are nearer to Europe than any of the other Arab countries and have a very rich cultural history. They can mix coast and desert (and other experiences) in the same visit. The Ahaggar Mountains in southern Algeria are one of the greatest pieces of desert scenery, and the Roman sites in Libya are unequaled (although there is strong competition in Tunisia and Algeria). Algeria and Libya are not yet as popular as Tunisia and Morocco, but are trying to catch up and, given political stability, they should easily do so.

Africa south of the Sahara

Desert tourism in the southern Sahara had a brief window of development between about 1970 and 1989, but numbers then crashed during revolutions, civil, and international wars. Niger and Chad have superb desert scenery, and other attractions like the neolithic frescos in the Tassili Mountains or the great volcanoes and stranded populations of crocodiles in the Ennedi Mountains in Chad. One hopes for the sakes of their economies, and for the sake of tourists frustrated at being unable to see these things, that stability will soon allow a return to a more open economy. When and if these deserts do open up again to tourists, they will have to forget independent travel (unless they want to really rough it). Public transport is primitive; hire cars without a driver attached are virtually unknown. Roads are still rudimentary (there are no tarmac roads into any of these deserts), and infrastructure, like petrol stations, hotels, and restaurants, is rudimentary (which is in itself an attraction to many visitors).

Southern Africa, building on political stability, saw a rapid increase in tourism in the 1990s, including desert tourism. South Africa, Botswana, and Namibia have extensive and accessible arid tracts with grand landscapes and unique communities and cultures. Most of them also have excellent roads and efficient car-hire networks. On their margins are some of the richest of Africa's wildlife reserves.

Iran and Central Asia

The Iranian tourist industry is not in good shape, but intensive efforts to attract tourists from as far away as Australia and China may bear some fruit. There are some excellent facilities, some stunning landscapes, and extraordinary archaeological remains from various periods.

Central Asia, even 20 years ago, suffered the worst effects of centralized bureaucracy: appalling hotels; police scrutinizing every tourist party; requirements for reams of paperwork, like visas; restrictions on travel and so on. Some of the republics, like Tadjikistan, are still unsafe. Many still have very authoritarian regimes; some have environmental disasters (like the Aral Sea) that are best avoided, except by the extremely curious. The biggest draw to central Asia is the Old Silk Road, and there are many tours that use it as their main storyline. But the real attractions of the Road are approachable without the need for exhausting travel: they are the ancient desert cities of Tashkent, Samarkand, and Bokhara, where there are still stunningly beautiful mosques (carefully preserved by the Soviets) and an amazingly rich history. If one is brave enough, there is spectacular scenery to be seen among huge desert mountains and valleys.

China

China's main tourist attractions are not in its deserts, although some enterprising communities in the desert like Dunhuang on the eastern margin of its deserts; Kashi, a

▲ **Statue of a nomad** *and camels in Rejistan Square in Samarkand, Uzbekistan. Founded in around 700 BCE, Samarkand historically has been one of central Asia's principal cities; its location on the Silk Road ensured that the city prospered for much of its early history.*

huge oasis in the far west; Urumqi in the northwest, and Lhasa in Tibet are making attempts to attract tourists. None of them has a large tourist infrastructure and most of the tours on offer seem to be organized by some central authority. The Chinese deserts, of course, are not for quiet recreation, but for seeing some amazing natural and cultural monuments. Visiting them in winter is against most advice. China is open for individual travel, but most of it is strenuous. An enduring attraction, here as in Central Asia, is the Old Silk Road, whose many branches also reached across central Asia, to which there are many guidebooks. Desert wildlife, like the reintroduced Przewalski's horse, or the less rare wild bactrian camels, is more difficult to see, but worth the attempt.

India and Pakistan

Today Rajasthan, in western India, is not only very accessible, but offers tourists a huge range of options as regards accommodation and travel. Its main attractions are cultural rather than natural. The far west of the country, near the Pakistan border, is true desert, with moving sand dunes, and with plenty of camel tours on offer. But most people remain in the ancient walled cities of Jaisalmer (close to the desert) and Jodhpur (farther away).

Australia

Australian deserts, like those in the United States are visited more by locals than foreigners. This means that, like the American deserts, the Australian deserts have excellent infrastructure for tourists: good roads, good and variously-priced hotels, good guidebooks, and tour guides. There is even a new railroad between Darwin and Adelaide, across the central desert. There are still huge spaces. The other attractions are great: unique wildlife, desert water holes, caves and waterfalls, canyons, huge rocks like Uluru. The disfigurements, as at vast opencast mines, are easily avoided.

North America

The North American deserts, particularly in the United States are probably the best known, and, in many respects also the best regulated of tourist destinations. The number of visitors each year to the Grand Canyon now tops five million, but the Parks Service confines the vast majority to the rims of the canyon and allows visits to the river itself only to a limited number of permit holders. There are many more such well-regulated places with remarkable scenery north, south, east and west of the Grand Canyon itself. The interest is not just geological, geomorphological, or botanical, as at the Joshua Tree National Park, or where there are giant Saguaro

▼ *Storm clouds* gather over Joshua trees at Joshua Tree National Park, California. The park is home to a number of desert animals, including sidewinder snakes, jackrabbits, kangaroo rats, and the aptly named stinkbug beetle.

cacti. More and more pre-Colombian settlements are being meticulously examined by archaeologists, and then opened to visitors. Roads are good, cars easy to hire, and organized tours with excellent interpretation are easy to access. Some tourists are appalled by Las Vegas or Palm Springs (each excessive in its own way), but visiting them is not obligatory.

Mexico also has its deserts, many very attractive, and with a uniquely ancient culture. One of them, on the peninsula of Baja California, has become very attractive to short- and long-term visitors. The attractions include amazing marine life (such as whales), and desert scenery. Some would add the fast-growing tourist towns to the list; others would see them as things to be suffered.

South America

Strictly speaking, a list of South American deserts should include the Peninsula of Venezuela, and the Caatinga in northeastern Brazil (where there are moving dunes as there should be in any good desert), but, to most people these are not real deserts or, at least, only in part.

▲ **Tourists** visiting the Caral archaeological complex in Peru. The ancient city has five pyramids—Mayor, Galery, Huyanca, Minor and Cantera—which are believed to be the remains of one of the oldest cities in the world.

The attractions in the Peruvian and Chilean coastal regions are very many: mountain scenery, wildlife (vicuñas and related camelid species) incredible colors in the higher deserts under clear skies; ancient drawings on the stony deserts; ancient oases watered by intricate pre-Colombian networks of channels; vast salars, or salt lakes, with flamingoes.

The high puna in parts of Chile and Bolivia is not for those who suffer altitude sickness, but it too is rich in wildlife and scenery. The Monte Desert in Argentina is an extension of the Atacama, but is more of a rain-shadow desert between high snow-capped peaks. It also has archaeological and ornithological attractions. Patagonia's attractions are in its mountains rather than its deserts, which are vast and gray.

THE ATLAS

From the great sand seas of the Sahara to the foggy coastal plains of Peru, from the broken rock of the cold Gobi to the searing volcanic heat of the Danakil, the variety of desert environments is greater even than the number of deserts themselves. The Atlas explores, region by region, the deserts of the world. It looks at the physical characteristics of the deserts and the great forces of nature that formed them. It describes the lives of the peoples who inhabit the deserts and their unique and extraordinary cultures. The resources of desert—both living and mineral—and how they are exploited are discussed, together with the threats to the ecologies and the people of the deserts and their margins.

THE WORLD'S DESERTS

Hot deserts comprise more than 30 percent of the Earth's land surface. They cover very high proportions of the continents of Africa and Australia, and almost all of southwest Asia and Central Asia, as well as all of the southwestern states of the United States and much of northern Mexico. There are no deserts in Europe and only small parts of South America are desert (although these are particularly extreme in character).

The extent of desert regions is not fixed. Every year weather conditions vary. Periods of dry years may occur together and establish local patterns of aridity that may prevent the regeneration of natural vegetation and so affect the extents of deserts.

Deserts and remote sensing

The Atlas section of this book combines maps of the world's deserts with images taken by remote sensing satellites orbiting the Earth. Since the 1960s, the Earth has been scanned daily by satellites carrying cameras and other sensing devices. Since the 1970s there have also been geostationary platforms with sensors scanning the hemispheres of the globe every half-hour. The information captured by some of these sensors provides images closely resembling the true color photographs with which the eye is very familiar. However, most of the information recorded is from parts of the electromagnetic spectrum outside the visible wavelengths.

Unfortunately, there is no rational system for converting the huge volume of remotely sensed data into visible colors. At visible wavelengths, objects and surfaces that appear red in color are reflecting the red light that falls on them while at the same time absorbing the ultraviolet, blue, green and yellow parts of the spectrum. Vegetation, on the other hand, appears green because it absorbs red and other wavelengths and reflects green light. Vegetation also strongly reflects infrared light, but this light is invisible to the eye. Because infrared light is recorded by remote sensing systems and conveys information, it is important to be able to show this information on photographic images.

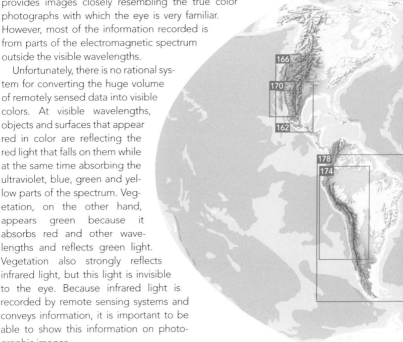

It is conventional to show infrared reflection in red, so in many of the pictures in the Atlas where heavily vegetated areas are present such vegetation appears red. Heavily cropped areas, such as the irrigated delta and valley of the Nile, thus show in red. In the wet season, marginal areas, such as the Sahel region of Africa, will show as versions of red according to the degree of vegetation cover present in that particular year. Satellite imagery is very useful for recording land surface changes both during a season and from year to year and make an important source of information on the controversial issue of desertification.

The spectacular imagery contained in the section that follows exemplifies the capability of remote sensing to provide information about vast areas. However, satellite images can record information other than the presence and absence of vegetation, and the varying geology of desert regions. Satellite-borne sensors can also record temperature and soil moisture, and meteorological satellites record the weather systems that determine both the terrestrial and ocean environments, including those of the world's deserts.

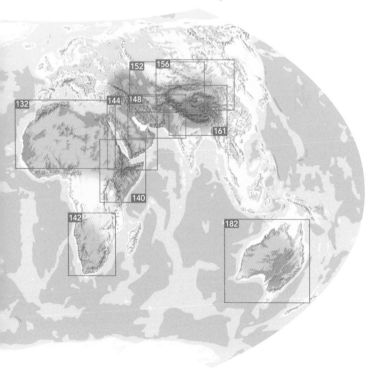

THE SAHARA

The Sahara is the world's largest desert, a wilderness of stony plains, mountains, rocky plateaus, and immense sand seas, stretching from the Red Sea in the east to the Atlantic Ocean in the west, and from the southern shore of the Mediterranean to about 10° latitude. The Sahara (depending on how one defines it) covers 3.5 million square miles (9 million square kilometers), and parts are claimed by 10 states.

Such a huge area inevitably includes a range of climates. The great, hyper-arid core of the desert has immensely hot summers, when temperatures can reach well over 130°F (55°C) in the shade. In places like Kufrah, in Libya, or Taoudenni, in Mali, it may not rain for years on end. On the northern fringes it is not uncommon to see hoarfrost on the dunes on a winter morning, and even the southern edges are chilly in winter. In the core, away from the few oases, there is virtually no vegetation, except in some of the larger wadis, where a few acacia trees may survive. Moving north out of the desert, one encounters more and more grassland, and then low scrub. Moving south, sparse grass, low widely dispersed scrub, and then trees appear. In this southern zone, a new hazard intrudes: the strong *harmattan* wind of February,

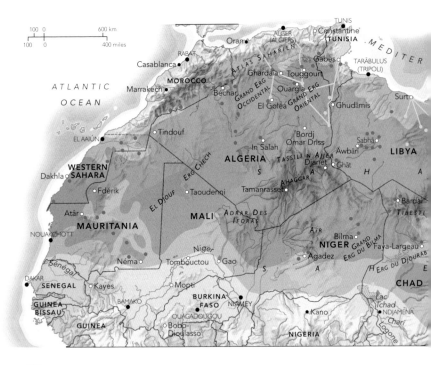

March, April and early May takes dust from the now-dry bed of a huge Pleistocene lake—Lake Mega-Chad—and blows it southwestward over the whole of West Africa and then over to the Amazon basin. The *harmattan* season is not a nice time to be in the Sahel: the Sun is obscured by dust; it gets into the lungs and may bring diseases like meningitis. Farther west, another source of dust feeds another stream of dust that travels over to Barbados and even to Florida in the United States. In contrast, the summits of the Aïr and Tibesti are quite cool, even cold, especially in winter and support a few bushes of Mediterranean flora.

The landscape

Although underlain by a much-eroded block of very ancient rock, the Sahara contains an astonishing variety of landscapes. In the center are the two massive volcanic blocks of the Ahaggar and Tibesti. The volcanic cones are still preserved in the Tibesti, but all that remains in the Ahaggar are the great fluted pillars of the lava plugs that were the cores of the volcanic cones. The volcanic rocks rest on ancient sandstone plateaux, which connect the Ahaggar and Tibesti massifs and occur in many other parts of the central Sahara. Some are quite prominent features like the Tassili n' Ajjer in Algeria and Libya, the Ennedi massif in Chad, and the Gilf el Kebîr in Egypt. Other, lower mountain massifs, like the Aïr mountains in Niger and Uweinat on the borders of Egypt and Libya, are uplifted portions or very hard rocks of the ancient basement.

Between these higher areas there are broad, stony, nearly featureless plains, knows as *serir* (or *sarir*). The two largest are the Sarir Calanscio in Libya and the Tanezrouft in Algeria and Mali (crossed each year by the Paris-Dakaar rally). Each of these is as big as France, and can take days to drive across. There are also some huge sand sheets like the El Wâhât el Selîma (Selîma Sand Sheet) in southern Egypt and northern Sudan, beneath which radar imagery from space has discovered the courses of very ancient rivers.

Sand seas cover one-third of the Sahara. In the Issouane n' Irararrene in Algeria, some dunes reach 400 feet (122 meters) in

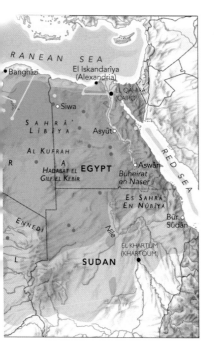

Desert

Semiarid

Lakes

—— Rivers

✦ Mining/mineral exploration

○ Oil and gas fields

—— Oil pipelines

● Oasis

● Capital cities

● Large cities

○ Other important towns/settlements

—— International boundaries

height. The greatest sand seas, or *ergs*, are in the north, notably the Grand Erg Oriental and the Grand Erg Occidental in Algeria, the Idehan Marzūk in Libya and the great sand seas of Egypt's Western Desert. The Grand Erg Oriental covers 74,000 square miles (192,000 square kilometers). Between the shifting dunes, long corridors of rocky or coarse sandy soil carry the caravan routes, and preserve the remains of lakes that filled the hollows in wetter times and of the prehistoric people who depended on them.

Human settlement

The Sahara was much better watered than it is now repeatedly during human prehistory. Some anthropologists refer to its wetting and drying as the "Saharan pump"—the Sahara pulled in Palaeolithic people when it was wet, and repulsed them when it was dry. Only the remains of the people who lived there in the wet periods are found today. Remains of the intervening cultures, when the Sahara was dry are absent. Nevertheless the remains are so thick on the ground in some parts of the Sahara, that it appears that every tenth stone is a tool or a flake. Neolithic people left fish-hooks in areas where rainfall is now seldom even an annual event, pottery, and beautiful cave paintings. The bed of ancient Lake Chad is strewn with the bones of crocodiles, whose modern relatives survive only in a few pools in the nearby Ennedi Mountains. There is evidence of many other large lakes, though none as big, all over the Sahara. About 4000 BCE, the Sahara began to turn arid again.

▲ *The Sahara Desert covers an area roughly equal to that of the United States. Dune fields (erg), cover only part of the total surface; the rest of the landscape consists of reg (wind-scoured gravel plains), hammada (rocky plateaux with deeply eroded gorges) or mountains such as the Ahaggar, the Aïr or the Tibesti.*

Saharan resources
Water

The Sahara is a hostile environment. Rainfall is too scarce to support crops, and even livestock rearing is not generally a viable activity. This barren environment can barely support wildlife, livestock, or people, and the flora and fauna that do exist have had to adapt dramatically in order to survive. Human communities of the Sahara throughout history have developed a range of remarkable and inventive strategies in their struggle for survival.

The Sahara is crossed by one major river, the Nile; the Niger touches its southern boundary, but then veers away again; some other perennial rivers hardly penetrate its borders (such as the Logone and Chari that feed Lac Tchad (Lake Chad); and yet others are ephemeral (flowing only at some seasons and in some years), like the Oued Saoura in Algeria. These rivers support the four-fifths or more of the human population. This leaves the great spaces of the Sahara as one of the emptiest regions on Earth.

With surface water so scarce and unreliable, groundwater has always been enormously significant in the Sahara. Much of the groundwater of the Sahara is of very high quality and suitable both for agricultural and domestic uses. But more than half of the exploitable water is ancient water, which fell as rain many thousands of years ago. Dating of the water in the biggest of the aquifers, in the Nubian Sandstone of the northeastern Sahara, show that the deepest water is between 200,000 to 1,200, 000 years old, and the water held above 1,600 feet (600 meters) below the surface is about 160,000 years old. The aquifers must have been filled when the Sahara was much wetter than it is today. These water resources, therefore, are finite, or "fossil." Once used, they will not replenish (or at least not until the next wet period, whenever that may be). The major aquifer beneath Algeria and southern Tunisia, in the Continental Intercalaire formation, is recharged from the meager rains that fall on, and gradually filter down into, this vast reserve, but that recharge is very slow.

The most spectacular development of Saharan groundwater retrieval was carried out in Libya during the 1980s and the 1990s. At this time, the water was used only in

▼ *In a bid to become more self-sufficient in meeting the country's need for wheat, Saudi Arabia has used its vast oil revenues to create artificial wheat fields in the middle of the desert. Around 0.6 mi (1 km) in diameter, the fields are irrigated using irreplaceable fossil water.*

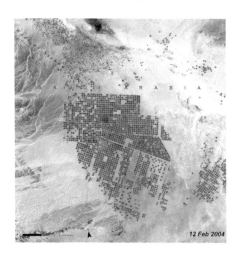

12 Feb 2004

the Kufrah area and in Fezzan. Now two huge pipelines (parts of the "Great Manmade River Project"), each large enough to drive a lorry along, take the water to the Mediterranean coast. Along the way, center-pivot irrigation systems have been set up, in which crops are grown in what before was completely unvegetated desert. Some estimates of the reserve give this scheme 100 years before the water runs out. Others claim 500 years. The Nubian aquifer also underlies parts of Egypt, where it is already exploited for irrigation, and Sudan and Chad, where it has yet to be tapped.

Mineral resources

In economic terms, minerals are the Sahara's most important natural resource. There are large reserves of oil in the Libyan and Algerian Sahara. Both countries derive more than 90 percent of their export earnings from these hydrocarbons. Tunisia and Egypt also have benefited from oil, but to a much smaller extent.

Other mineral resources have been, and remain, major contributors to the economies of some Saharan countries. Phosphates, for example, are Tunisia's major export, and while Morocco, Mauritania, and Western Sahara are also major phosphate producers, the stability of these exports has been disrupted by the insecurity and military activity of their border zones. Iron ore resources are also significant, especially in Mauritania.

Huge amounts of sunshine fall on the region throughout the year, and the Sahara's vast land area gives it the greatest potential for solar energy development of all the world's deserts. The problem is not so much the technology for solar energy conversion, which has been becoming much more sophisticated, but because of its price relative to the prices of fossil energy. However, with the costs of fossil energy rising at a very steep rate (in 2006) solar technology may well become competitive quite soon. The northern Sahara is already connected to a European grid, and experiments in feeding this grid with solar energy may happen quite soon. What effects this would have on Saharan economies is debatable. At another scale solar energy, when it becomes competitive, might transform life in the Sahara: it could be used for local supplies (as it already widely is in telecommunications), but also to drive pumps to raise water, or to desalinate brackish waters (where even with fossil energy at its present price, it can be a competitive way to supply fresh water). At the moment, capital costs and maintenance are large issues preventing the penetration of this technology.

The Tuareg

When the Arab armies moved across North Africa in the 11th century CE, they replaced the Berbers as the ruling population. While much of the Berber population was and remains sedentary, some were nomadic. The best known of these are the Tuareg, whose indigo-robed male warriors provide one of the Sahara's most familiar images. After the first Arab conquests, the Tuareg were initially reluctant to adopt Islam, but over the following centuries this reluctance was replaced by a devout adherence. Tuareg men must wear a veil, known as the *tagilmust* (a long strip of cotton, often dyed blue). Women wear a smaller veil, which covers only the mouth.

The Tuareg number around one million, and are divided into seven groups or confederations. Their homeland lies in six states: Mali, Burkina Faso, Mauritania, Niger, Algeria, and Libya. For centuries they have followed a nomadic or semi-nomadic way of life, based on the raising of camels, goats, sheep, and cattle.

The Tuareg speak dialects of Tamahaq, itself a form of Senhadjan Berber. Dialects vary according to the tribal confederation. The Ahaggar Tuareg confederation is itself broadly divided into three tribes: the Kela Rela, Tégéhé Millet, and the Taituq. Each tribe is headed by a clan, distinguished as aristocrats. Traditional Tuareg society consisted of three classes: nobles, vassals, and slaves. Historically, Tuareg nobles controlled the Saharan caravan routes. The vassals concentrated on herding. The slaves and former slaves, knows as *harratin*, performed menial duties, including looking after oasis agriculture, and guarded tribal encampments.

Tuareg culture is patriarchal, but inheritance of the chieftainship of the tribe passes through the female line, so that the successor is the eldest son of the incumbent's eldest sister. Tribal succession has always been a pragmatic affair, determined by the willingness of the clan to pay tribute to the leader, the *amenukal*.

Tuareg traditions have suffered under economic and political pressures in recent years. Originally,

▼ *A Tuareg nomad* prepares tea for the caravan. For centuries, Tuareg nobles provided guides for Saharan camel caravans, which were the sole means of contact between the Mediterranean coastal regions and sub-Saharan Africa.

their traditions developed in a fluid fashion, because of the difficulty in maintaining strict social divisions and hierarchies among highly mobile nomadic groups. The Ahaggar confederation has been forced to break up the clan and tribal divisions into smaller familial groups because the intense aridity of the area requires quick movement between water supplies and grazing areas.

In addition to the pastoralist or herding economy, Tuareg tribes have long acted as intermediaries for cross-Saharan traffic. For long periods, Tuareg nobles controlled many of the trading routes across the Sahara, supplying guides for the Arab traders of the North African coastal region.

Mechanization has eliminated many of the problems of desert transport, depriving the Tuareg of their main source of external income. In addition, the Tuareg are now suffering the immediate effects of the long drought of the 1970s and 1980s. This situation has forced many of them to settle in towns.

A threatened people

Twentieth-century Tuareg history saw three military uprisings. The first, in the early years of the century, was easily suppressed by the French. They were the last North African people to sign treaties with the colonial powers (in 1905 and 1917). Little further political activity was permitted until the partition of the traditional Tuareg homelands of Aïr and Azawad between the newly independent states of Mali, Burkina Faso, Mauritania, Niger, Algeria, and Libya.

During the late 1970s, Colonel Muammar al Qadhafi, the Libyan leader, began to recruit Tuareg guerrillas to fight in Chad. As a result, many Tuareg began to pursue the dream of freeing the Azawad. In Mali and Niger, groups of Tuareg fighters then waged a guerrilla war against the governments of the countries whose boundaries crossed their homelands. Many thousands are thought to have been killed. Their demands varied from the total independence of the Aïr and Azawad, to greater regional autonomy. That war ended in 1992 in Mali and in 1995 in Niger (although there have been outbreaks of guerrilla warfare since), and Tuareg have made some sort of accommodation with the existing national governments. Their music, a sign of cultural persistence, has become well known in Europe.

▼ *Tuareg tribesmen* are *fiercely independent. Modern political boundaries cutting across the old caravan routes and destroying their traditional way of life have resulted in the Tuareg fighting for a state of their own.*

In "The Horn" there are deserts (as we have defined them) in Kenya, Somalia, Ethiopia, Djibouti, and Eritrea. The vast deserts of northern Sudan (which is sometimes included in The Horn) are essentially part of the Sahara.

Somali and Kenyan deserts

There are arid deserts in northern and eastern Kenya in which the main land use is pastoral. Various nomadic and semi-nomadic groups, including the Boran, the Gabbra, the Turkana and Somali clans, herd cattle, goats, sheep, and camels. Most people live in the few hill areas, like Mount Kulal, where the climate is wetter and more temperate, and where some agriculture can be undertaken. Lake Turkana, which covers 3,000 square miles (7,500 square kilometers), is a very alkaline lake in the midst of a very arid volcanic landscape, in which the remains some of the earliest hominid species have been found. Despite its alkalinity, Lake Turkana supports a small fishery. In northeastern Kenya, and extending into Somalia and southern Ethiopia, are the Chalbi and Didi Galgalu deserts

Parts of southeastern Somalia are watered by the Giuba and Scebeli rivers, along which there are settled agricultural groups and the densest populations in the country. Parts of the northern Highlands are also better watered and support a population of agriculturalists. The driest parts of the Horn are to the east of this zone in far eastern Somalia, Djibouti, and eastern Ethiopia, many parts being virtually uninhabited. The Ogaden Desert, in central Somalia is bounded to the west by the highlands of the Rift Valley. The population of the Ogaden consists almost entirely of nomadic herders, who suffer severely in droughts. Severe droughts happen every few years, and now appear to be related to ENSO (El Niño—Southern Oscillation) cycles in the Pacific.

A civil war in Somalia began in 1977 and has not ended, making the country ungovernable. In early 2006 it had no recognized government. The north (a former British colony) has declared unilateral secession and calls itself "Somaliland." A national assembly, of sorts, meets in Nairobi, where it is safer. It may manage its first meeting in Somalia itself in February 2006. The war has compounded the famines. At the same time, famine leads to political instability, in a vicious downward spiral.

The Danakil

In the northeast of Ethiopia, the Rift Valley opens out into a desert that extends into Djibouti to the east and Eritrea to the west. This has been known in the west for a long time as the Danakil Desert, although its people prefer to be called

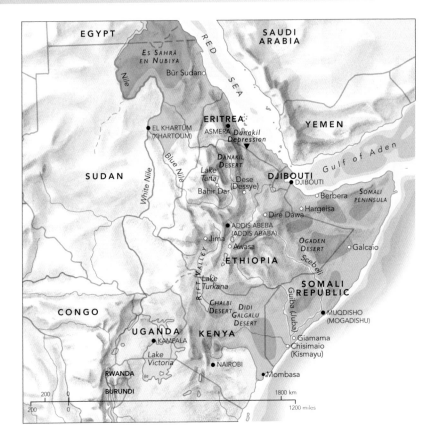

"Afar." This desert includes a depression that is about 400 feet (120 meters) below sea level. The Danakil is scorchingly hot, and the little rain it receives evaporates very quickly to leave large salt flats in depressions where water tends to gather. Active volcanoes belch out smoke and sulfurous fumes, and hot springs bubble, often with waters strangely colored by minerals.

The only relief in this fierce landscape is where the River Awash crosses the southern part of the region, creating a narrow fertile strip. The river evaporates, or disappears into its bed before reaching the sea, leaving only saltpans. The few inhabitants are the Afar herders, known for their ferocious protection of the few resources that the region has to offer. As in northern Kenya, the Danakil has yielded evidence of early ancient hominid species, including the famous "Lucy" who lived beside large lakes in a wetter climate.

■ Desert
▨ Semiarid
▨ Lakes
— Rivers
● Capital cities
● Large cities
○ Other important towns/settlements
— International boundaries

Most of the Kalahari is not strictly speaking a desert, as we have defined the word. However, it is desert in the sense of being lightly populated and in having very few permanent water sources (apart from boreholes). The southwestern Kalahari is true desert. This is the area in which South Africa, Namibia, and Botswana meet, with a complex set of borders. This desert stretches northwestward through Namibia towards the coast, where it joins with the hyperarid Namib Desert. The area is generally a very level plain covered with great swarms of writhing linear dunes interspersed with pans. These are wind-eroded basins in which water collects after rains. The dunes are only active at their low summits; the hollows between are vegetated. Some believe that this is one of the areas most vulnerable to climate change, which is likely to bring much drier climates and to reactivate the dunes, perhaps even in northern Botswana and eastern Namibia.

The Namib

The Namib Desert covers a narrow coastal strip in Namibia, northwestern South Africa and southern Angola, which seldom reaches beyond 90 miles (140 kilometers) from the shore. The Namib is separated from the moister highland plateau of Namibia by the Great Escarpment, a zone of hilly country that falls away steeply from the upland plain of Namibia at 2,600 feet (800 meters) and more. The perennial Orange River separates the South African parts of the Namib from the Namibian. It runs through a deep gorge, and is inaccessible for irrigation. The same is true of the Cunene River that separates Namibia from Angola to the north. The Namib can be said to extend for a few hundred miles north into Angola beyond the border.

The Namib is the classic hyperarid desert, but with the distinction that its shores (like those in Chile, Peru, Baja California, and Oman) is bathed in a cool oceanic current. The cool current off the Namib is the Benguela Current, which helps to maintain the aridity of the Namib. More than that, when winds blow off the cool current onto the warmer land, fog forms, keeping the coast cool in summer and maintaining a unique flora and fauna. Annual rainfall at Gobabeb, about 40 miles (60 kilometers) inland, is around 1 inch (25 millimeters), but it also receives round 1 inch (30 millimeters) of precipitation from fog, on an average of 37 days per year. The cool seas are (or were) also rich in fish, and there are commercial fisheries at Walvis Bay (until 1994 a South African enclave). There are reports of very serious overfishing in these seas.

South of the Kuiseb River, there is an area of huge, rose-red linear and star-shaped dunes—among the largest in the world. For most of the year, the Kuiseb is dry, but it flows often enough to prevent the northward movement of the dunes. The river does not flow every year and has not reached the sea

since 1933. North of the Kuiseb, there are gravel plains with occasional, very steep-sided mountains, known as *inselbergs* ("island mountains"), and some more massive mountain ranges.

Exploitation of the Namib

The Namib is too dry for permanent settlement (although holiday villages are springing up between Walvis Bay and Swakopmund (an old German settlement). However, mining companies have exploited the Namib's mineral wealth, first for diamonds (in the south) and more recently for uranium (in one of the world's largest uranium mines). For many years, large parts of the coastal strip were closed areas, controlled exclusively by the mining companies, but the whole of the coastal strip has now been declared a national park, which extends into South Africa and Angola.

Wildlife of the Namib

The Namib is remarkable for its great diversity of animal and plant species. Most notable is the beetle population, many species of which are found only in the Namib and thrive on the moisture provided by the fogs. Around 50 species of tenebrionid beetle rely on this moisture. Some dig trenches to catch moisture, others catch condensation on their bodies. This requires the beetle to be active often at the coldest part of the day—not easy for a cold-blooded creature. The beetle population provides food for lizards, geckos, snakes, gerbils, and golden moles, which then become the prey of larger animals. The sparse vegetation supports ostriches and antelope species such as springbok and oryx. Within the river valleys, carnivores such as hyenas and jackals may be found. The Namib is almost unique in supporting a population of desert elephants.

▶ *A tenebrinoid beetle* drinks condensed dew from the surface sand of the Namib Desert.

143

THE ARABIAN PENINSULA

The Arabian Desert extends south from the Euphrates River to the port of Aden on the Yemeni coast, and from the Jordanian port of Al Aqabah in the west to the headland of Ra's al-Had on the Omani coast in the east. From this vast desert area, covering some 900,000 square miles (2.3 million square kilometers), have come some of the most important influences on the world's culture and society. The region now contains two-thirds of the world's major energy resources (as oil) and includes, not surprisingly, some of the most heavily disputed territory in the world.

▨	Desert
▨	Semiarid
▨	Lakes
—	Rivers
●	Oil and gas fields
⁓	Oil pipelines
●	Oasis
●	Capital cities
●	Large cities
○	Other important towns/settlements
—	International boundaries

Physical characteristics

The Great Rift Valley splits at the head of the Red Sea with its two arms forming the edges of the Sinai Peninsula. The eastern arm runs northwards between Israel and Jordan, dropping down to the lowest point on Earth's land surface at the Dead Sea and fading out in Syria, causing the mountains west of Dimashq (Damascus). The eastern flank of the Rift Valley rises to form uplands in western Jordan, Saudi Arabia, and Yemen.

Beyond these bordering highlands, the desert drops away to the plains and sand deserts of the center, east, and south, which from nine-tenths of the entire area of the peninsula. This region seldom rises above 1,600 feet (500 meters). The far west of the peninsula is also uplifted in the geologically complex Oman Mountains, which were formed by the movement of an ancient sea floor over the platform of rock from which the peninsula is formed.

The platform is separated from the African continent by the rifts of the Red Sea and the Gulf of Aden. This ancient platform is covered on the eastern and central desert by layers of more recent rocks. These rocks characterize the Najd, or Central Plateau. This region is the homeland of Saudi Arabia's ruling Saud dynasty and the strict Muslim Wahhabi sect, whose *Ulama*, or senior clerics, rule the peninsula in conjunction with the Saudi royal family.

The southeastern peninsula is dominated by the intense heat and aridity of the sandy Rub' al Khālī, or Empty Quarter. The absence of rainfall and

▼ **A satellite image** of the Sinai Peninsula. Located entirely within Egypt, the 20,000 sq mi (60,000 km^2) area is almost entirely desert.

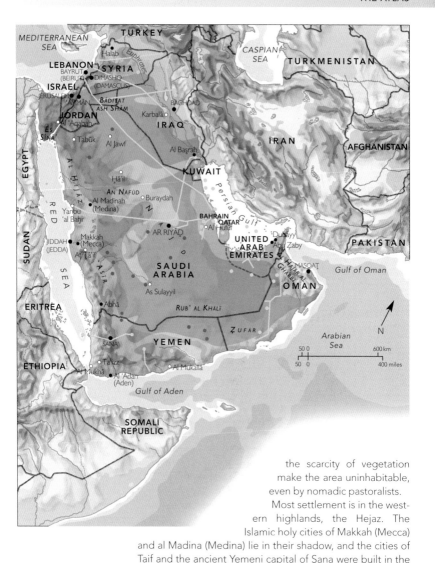

the scarcity of vegetation make the area uninhabitable, even by nomadic pastoralists.

Most settlement is in the western highlands, the Hejaz. The Islamic holy cities of Makkah (Mecca) and al Madina (Medina) lie in their shadow, and the cities of Taif and the ancient Yemeni capital of Sana were built in the highlands away from the heat of the plains.

Rainfall in Arabia is sparse and erratic, except in the western highlands. Summer temperatures in the Najd can reach 120°F (49°C), while around the coastal areas this drops to about 90°F (32°C). During the winter months—November to April—temperatures are a little lower, and can occasionally plummet to freezing at night.

145

Herding and agriculture

The Asir region in the southwest of the peninsula is the most fertile area. Here, farmers have created terraced fields on which they grow a variety of crops. The eastern lowlands, which back onto the Persian Gulf, have a number of oases which also support large agricultural settlements. Cattle, goats, and sheep provide the nomads and seminomads with, among other things, dairy products and meat.

Oil in the Middle East

The Arabian Peninsula lies on the block known as the Arabian plate, which is bounded by the African, Somali, and Eurasian plates. Its oldest rocks date back some 4,600 million years, but it is chalky sediments from the Mesozoic era (225–70 million years ago) that give the region its large oil reservoirs. These were formed when marine sediments were deposited in the Tethys Sea, which lay between the prehistoric "super-continents" of Gondwana and Laurasia.

More than 50 percent of the world's proven reserves of oil come from 33 "supergiant" fields of more than 5 billion barrels each; 28 of these lie in the Middle East, including nine of the ten largest. Most of the region's oil fields lie along the east coast of the peninsula and in the Persian Gulf.

Apart from oil and natural gas, the countries of the Arabian peninsula have very few other resources. There is some salt production, and there are limited quantities of zinc, lead, iron ore, copper, gold, and chromite. With the exception of the southeast, low rainfall throughout the region means that agriculture is possible only through irrigation.

The impact of oil

The development of oil and natural gas has been the driving force behind the economies of the Arabian peninsula. Industry in the peninsula depends almost entirely on the refining and processing of oil, or on the cheap energy that abundant oil provides. Oil has also brought far-reaching and radical change to the societies of the sparsely populated desert states. A way of life built around herding and nomadism has now largely given way to a more settled, urban lifestyle.

The massive oil price rises of the 1970s brought a huge inflow of revenues to the oil states. The development, however, has a high price because it comes largely not from productive enterprise but from a non-renewable resource.

Although oil revenues have resulted in the establishment of some of the most modern industry and welfare structures in the world, the domestic labor force alone was too small

▶ *A satellite image* of Dubayy's (Dubai's) latest ambitious building project. Known collectively as the Palm, the group of manmade islands supports luxury hotels and apartment blocks, marinas, shops, and movie theaters. Two further artificial island projects are planned, and the hope is that these, together with other mainland building proposals, will make Dubayy the number one tourist destination in the world.

and unskilled to accomplish this task. Foreign workers were recruited, initially from the Arab world, but increasingly from southern and eastern Asia.

Oil reserves

With proven reserves of 258 billion barrels, Saudi Arabia is the region's major producer. Oil was discovered in 1938 and development began after the Second World War. Among Saudi Arabia's most significant onshore oilfields are Al-Qatif, Berri Khurays, and Fadhili. There is also a number of extensive offshore fields.

Kuwait's first oil strike was also in 1938, and proven reserves are approximately 97 billion barrels. Kuwait's oil attracts lower prices on world markets, however, because it has a high specific gravity and a high sulfur content. Environmental considerations mean that lighter, cleaner crude oil is now increasingly preferred.

The United Arab Emirates (UAE) are major producers and have reserves of 98 billion barrels. Most of this lies in Abū Ζāby, although Dubayy (Dubai) has a number of offshore fields. The other, smaller emirates have some reserves of gas. Other Arab states have smaller reserves. Qatar has about 5 billion barrels, but it also has vast reserves of natural gas.

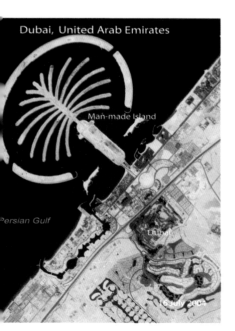

Dubai, United Arab Emirates

Man-made Island

Persian Gulf

Dubai

16 July 2004

Oman's first discoveries were not made until 1964. Oil reserves are modest at just over 4 billion barrels. Yemen's discoveries in the 1990s have been very important in ameliorating the worst features of its poorly developed economy, but they will only last for between one and two decades of the 21st century.

Awareness of the impact of oil pollution was heightened by the 1991 Kuwait Gulf War. Pollution was already severe in the Persian Gulf. It was worsened by the events of the earlier Iran-Iraq war of 1980–88. In 1991, Iraqi forces released an estimated 4 to 6 million barrels of oil into the Gulf during the Gulf War, with disastrous effect on the wildlife of the region. Inland, 150 million barrels of oil leaked into the desert from wellheads sabotaged by the Iraqis; this has already contaminated soils and vegetation and may seep into groundwater supplies.

Most of the interior of Iran is a plateau surrounded by mountain ranges. The plateau, all of which is over 1,650 feet (500 meters) above sea level, is divided into two major areas: the salt desert, or Dasht-e Kavīr is an inhospitable region, parts of which are completely uninhabitable. Salt plasters the surface, rendering cultivation impossible, and in places even travel is hazardous. Salt crusts cover areas of mud which conceal deep subterranean channels. The fragile structure of the surface is extremely dangerous.

The Dasht-e Lūt is very different to the Dasht-e Kavīr, being largely covered with loose sand and desert pavement (small stones). Both regions, however, suffer from extremes of climate. Summer temperatures reach over 122°F (50°C), while the winter temperature can drop below freezing. The temperature variation in the central Iranian plain is exacerbated by the high winds common to the area.

Average annual rainfall exceeds 24 inches (600 millimeters) only in the highlands of the western and north margins. In the central plateau, rain is much more scarce, with an annual average of 8 inches (200 millimeters) in the southeast and less than 4 inches (100 millimeters) elsewhere.

Tehran

Tehran, the capital of Iran, encapsulates the environmental problems of urban settlement on the fringe of the desert. The city lacks an easily available water source and has long since exceeded its supposed maximum population of 5.5 million, identified by a development plan in the 1970s. An influx of people from the countryside, something that has occurred elsewhere in the Middle East, is just one of the factors that has caused the city's population to rise to over 8 million. The severe overpopulation that has occurred in urban areas of Iran, and in Tehran in particular, has led to a reduction in the available clean water supplies in many areas of the country.

The Great Indian Desert

Pakistan and India are separated by a vast natural barrier, the Thar, or Great Indian, Desert. The Thar covers an area of some 77,000 square miles (200,000 square kilometers) and is well known for its sand dunes, some of which can reach a height of 500 feet (150 meters).

Desert
Semiarid
Lakes
Rivers
♦ Mining/mineral exploration
Oil and gas fields
Oil pipelines
● Capital cities
● Large cities
○ Other important towns/settlements
International boundaries

Average annual rainfall in the region ranges from about 4 inches (100 millimeters) in the west, to 20 inches (500 millimeters) in the east. The lack of rain, combined with high temperatures and strong winds of up to 90 miles (150 kilometers) per hour, particularly in May and June, not only creates frightening sand storms, but also leads to fertile soil often being covered over with sand. Unlike many deserts, the Thar also lacks a good groundwater resource. What little groundwater there is lies very deep and is usually too saline to be useful.

Because of these harsh factors and summer temperatures of 122°F (50°C) very few people formerly lived in the region. Those who did raised sheep and cattle in small areas where there was sufficient water for grass. However, with the completion of the huge Indira Gandhi Canal scheme in 1986, several irrigation projects have been constructed. These have attracted settlers and pastoralists to the region.

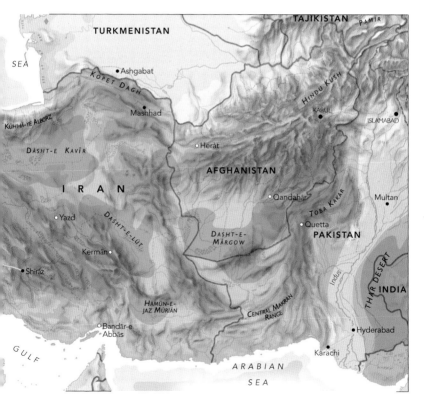

Nationality and religion

The human and political landscape of the Middle East is a constantly changing, unstable mix of religions and national identities. This blend has contributed to numerous wars and movements of people, as well as a legacy of international disputes such as the Arab-Israeli conflict. Some of the most hotly disputed areas are also among the emptiest, but their oil fields have made them the focus of global strategic interest. A dispute between Iraq and Kuwait over the Burgan oil field was one factor that led to the Gulf War of 1991.

The Middle East saw the birth of three major monotheistic religions—Islam, Christianity, and Judaism—that are still important today. Until the rise of Islam in the 7th century CE, Christianity was the religion of much of the region. However, the Middle East has always been very divided, if only by the vast, inhospitable distances between peoples, and Christianity never exerted much influence over the desert nomads of Arabia. Islam itself is divided into two main branches, each subdivided into numerous sects.

National identity

Nationality is a term more difficult to define than religion. It may denote ancient communities, such as the Egyptians and Persians, or it may indicate countries such as Libya and Jordan that have only recently come into existence. Lebanon's mosaic of sects, communities, and clans was given national status after World War I to further Western political goals in the region. Iraq's Kurdish minority represent a nation in terms of their common language, culture, and homeland, whereas religious identity and practice distinguish the Shiite Muslims in the marshes of southeast Iraq from their fellow Iraqis.

The Middle East is, above all, the home of the Arab people. The Arabs are united by a common language and heritage, but are divided into a northern, Mediterranean group claiming descent from Adnan, and the South Arabian group found in Yemen, the Hadhramaut and Oman. This distinction was perpetuated in the days of the Arab empire, leading to civil strife and dynastic conflict. The decline of the Ottoman Empire in the early 20th century enabled Arab nationalism to flourish. By the end of World War II, most of the Arab states had won their independence. During the 1960s, the Egyptian president, Gamal Abdel Nasser, led the unsuccessful drive for Arab political unity known as Pan-Arabism. Some Muslims dream of an age which will bring about the demise of nationality through the achievement of a grand pan-Islamic vision. Many Arabs still dream of creating some form of pan-Arab state.

▼ *An Iranian woman visits a cemetery for the victims of the Iran-Iraq War. The conflict began on September 22, 1980, when Iraq invaded Iran following a series of border disputes between the two countries. After eight years of attritional fighting and over one million casualties, the war ground to a halt and the two countries' borders were left unchanged.*

Modern Israel is a very recent state, coming into existence officially in 1948, yet it enshrines Jewish dreams of a return to the homeland that date back 2,000 years. Within Israel, there are long-existing Arab Muslim, Christian, and Druze minorities who are Israeli by nationality, but whose loyalties may lie elsewhere. About 75 percent of the Israeli population reflects early 20th-century immigration augmented by that of the late 1940s and 1950s. Immigration from the former Soviet Union during the late 1980s and early 1990s increased the proportion of the immigrant population to 80 percent. As a result of Israel's occupation of the West Bank of the Jordan River (including eastern Jerusalem) and the Gaza Strip during the Six-Day War of 1967, Israel still dominates a rebellious Palestinian Arab population, who also cherish dreams of nationhood.

Militant Islam

Islam is divided into two branches: Sunni and Shia. Sunni Muslims represent 80 percent of the Islamic world, but Shiites predominate in Iran. In 1979, the rise of Shiite militancy in Iran led to the overthrow of the Western-backed monarch, the Shah, and the establishment of a religious government led by the *imam* (religious leader) the Ayatollah Khomeini. Iran's Islamic revolution sent shockwaves throughout the Persian Gulf region.

Iraq has a Shiite minority which is Arab, but their Shiite neighbors in Iran are Persian, which can often bring about a conflict of religious and national loyalties. Meanwhile, in largely Sunni Afghanistan, ethnic divisions between the Pashto-speakers and the Persian-speaking Tajiks have lead to further divisiveness in the region.

Within nomadic communities, charismatic religious movements have led to religious and political changes. The Almoravid movement, which began among the Berber nomads of the Western Sahara in the 11th century, resulted in the building of a North African empire. In the 18th century, the puritanical Wahhabi sect arose amongst the Bedouins of the Najd region of the Arabian Peninsula. In time, it brought about the establishment of the present Saudi ruling house.

151

CENTRAL ASIA

Central Asia is covered by the five Asian republics of the former USSR, and occupies an area two-fifths the size of Europe. The region is fringed by the Russian Federation to the north, the Caspian Sea to the west, the Kopet-Dagh of Iran and Afghanistan to the south, and the Tien Shan, Pamir and Altay mountains to the south and east.

Most of the region consists of a depression containing the Aral and Caspian seas, and a series of plateaux and plains sloping to the Caspian, whose eastern shores have a number of salt lakes, the most notable of which is Garabogazköl Aylagy. There are two other major areas of water in the region: the Aral Sea and Balqash Köl (Lake Balkhash). Otherwise the terrain is mainly desert and semiarid subtropical terrain.

The two main deserts are the Kyzyl Kum (Red Sands) in Uzbekistan and the Garagum (Kara Kum or Black Sands) of Turkmenistan. There is also the Moyynqum Desert in south Kazakhstan and the Borsyk Desert north of the Aral Sea. The northern part of the Kyzyl Kum desert is a steppe area, which has its annual spring abundance of vegetation scorched off by the summer heat. The southern part is a semidesert plateau.

Amudarya and Syrdarya

The two main rivers in the region are the Amudarya and the Syrdarya, which rise in the mountains to the southeast of the region and flow generally northward to the Aral Sea. Extensive irrigation provided by these rivers has resulted in development of fertile land in the Fergana valley of east Uzbekistan, southern Kazakhstan, and the northern fringes of Kyrgyzstan descending to the Kazakhstan steppes. However, as rain is irregular, the Khorazm oasis at Khiva in Uzbekistan is being encroached upon by the desert, and many old watercourses have been dry for centuries.

Reservoirs have been created to secure expanding irrigation. A lake 3 miles (5 kilometers) long has been created at Bukhtarm on the upper stretches of the Irtysh in Kazakhstan, while the damming of the Amudarya at Khujand has formed another lake, the "Tajik Sea." Another notable artificial feature is the 850-mile (1,350-kilometer) Kara Kum Canal along the southern Turkmenistan border.

The region lies in the largest continent at a relatively northern latitude, and there is no barrier between it and the Arctic, resulting in cold winters and scorching summers. The snow of the mountain fringes feeds water sources with its runoff in the spring and summer. High winds, in combination with the desiccation of the Aral Sea, have caused serious salt storms in the region.

	Desert
	Semiarid
	Lakes
—	Rivers
♦	Mining/mineral exploration
•	Oil and gas fields

Oil pipelines
• Oasis
● Capital cities
● Large cities
○ Other important towns/settlements
— International boundaries

In the desert areas only the hardiest of vegetation can survive, for example, tamarisks (*Tamarix* spp.), the *kok sagyg* (which produces latex), and *solianka*, a bushy shrub with bright red flowers. The desiccation of the Aral Sea has resulted in increased salinity and this has caused the death of the 24 species of fish native to the sea. In addition, the boars (*Sus scrofa*), deer, and egrets that the Aral Sea once supported have also disappeared. In the fertile areas, the main vegetation is commercial crops—predominantly cotton—with substantial numbers of fruit trees in the Fergana Valley and melon crops growing along the main river valleys.

People and problems

Central Asia is a predominantly Muslim area, with native populations consisting mainly of Tadjik (Indo-European) and Turco-Mongol stock. There is also a sprinkling of Muslim Uigur people who fled from repression in northwestern China. Additionally, substantial groups of ethnic Germans from the Volga region, as well as Trans-Caucasians, Ukrainians, and Russians, resettled in Central Asia, particularly during the rule of Stalin, creating a very mixed population.

▲ *The Sun sets over the Kara Kum Canal, the longest irrigation waterway in the world. The canal carries 3 cu mi (13 km³) of water from the Amudarya River across the Garagum Sands to Ashgabat.*

Industry and agriculture

Economic activity is a mixture of agriculture, the mining and processing of a variety of minerals, and energy-production industry. The area is rich in mineral resources, with coal in the Qaraghandy (Karaganda) region of Kazakhstan, lead and zinc in the Aerhtai Shan (Altai mountains), iron and copper around Balqash Köi (Lake Balkhash) and Almalyk, and iron ore together with the associated production of steel in Tashkent.

The damming of the Syrdarya and Amudarya, and the creation of several artificial lakes have led to considerable production of hydroelectric power in the mountains, although this is still an under-developed resource. Oil and natural gas reserves are found throughout the region, especially in the Caspian and Bukhara areas of Uzbekistan and in Turkmenistan, and are also not exploited to their full potential.

The main crop is cotton—the "white gold"—which has made the region famous and drained its environment. The industry began in the 19th century when the American Civil War cut exports from North America, creating a European demand for cotton from other sources. New irrigation projects began in 1918, and by the time the Soviet Union came to an end, the cotton industry was producing two-thirds of all Soviet cotton. As the industry developed, however, it relied increasingly on intensive irrigation and heavy subsidies from central funds to maintain production.

The desiccation of the Aral Sea

As a result of irrigation projects, the Aral Sea lost about 40 percent of its surface area between 1960 and 1990,

▼ **The Aral Sea,** once home to a thriving fishing industry, has become an environmental catastrophe. Extensive areas of dry seabed are now exposed and the old shorelines are obscured by drifts of alluvial and wind-blown silt that now cover much of the landscape. The receding waters have left vast plains covered with salt and toxic chemicals, which are then blown over the surrounding region. This has resulted in a regional population that exhibits high rates of cancer, as well as respiratory and other diseases.

amounting to some 11,000 square miles (28,000 square kilometers). Diverting water for agriculture disturbed the balance between inflow to and evaporation from the sea. By 2004, the Aral Sea's surface area was a quarter of the size it was in 1960.

The desiccation of the Aral Sea poses a major environmental threat to the region and its population of 35 million people. The drop in the level of the sea has been accompanied by a corresponding drop in the quality of water. Furthermore, much land in the irrigated areas has been affected by salts rising to the surface in the naturally saline desert soil—a side effect of irrigation.

The northwestern region of Uzbekistan, which borders the Aral Sea, has suffered most directly from the environmental changes caused by the desiccation of the sea. There has been a significant increase in respiratory and eye diseases linked to the increasing amounts of salt and other sea-bed materials in the air. Childhood diseases associated with the increased aridity are also a problem.

The future of the Aral

The effects of desiccation have spread to many parts of the economy. The Qoraqalpog (Karakalpak) region once had a flourishing fishing and canning industry. As the sea receded so this industry failed and left the fishing centers landlocked. The problem of the Aral Sea is so great that drastic measures will have to be taken if it is not to dry completely. One solution suggested is to divert water from the Ob and the Irtysh rivers to feed the sea. Environmentalists are opposed to this because the scheme could compound the region's problems. More realistic are the projects to strengthen irrigation canals and use water more effectively. In addition, attempts are being made to save delta lakes and turn some into fish farms to salvage the fishing industry.

On top of problems caused by irrigation, the cotton-growing areas suffer from the heavy use of pesticides, which has restricted much of the land to cotton growing (rather than food crops) for safety reasons. The use of Butifos, which defoliates cotton plants for ease of picking, and the continued use of DDT, despite bans, had poisoned the land.

THE GOBI DESERT

The Gobi Desert is the world's fifth largest desert. It takes its name from the Mongolian word meaning "waterless place." The Gobi stretches across southeast Mongolia and northern China, covering an area of approximately 500,000 square miles (1,295,000 square kilometers), and extending 1,000 miles (1,610 kilometers) from east to west and 565 miles (910 kilometers) from north to south. Rainfall in the Gobi averages 2–4 inches (50–100 millimeters) annually, although it is higher in the northeast of the region. Temperatures vary from –40°F (–40°C) in January to 113°F (45°C) in July.

The Takla Makan

The Gobi actually comprises several distinct arid areas. In the west lies the Takla Makan (or Ka Shun) Desert. It is bounded by the Tian Shan range in the north and west, and the Kunlun Shan and Altun Shan to the south. The Takla Makan is a vast sea of dunes developed on an undulating, elevated plain, which rises to 5,000 feet (1,525 meters). The dunes are interspersed with a complex series of hills and scarps, which can rise 1,000 feet (300 meters) above the plain. Salty, dry lakes lie between the dunes, some of them eroded into fields of fantastic yardangs (wind-sculpted hillocks). Northeast of the Takla Makan lies the Pendi Junggar basin, nestling between the eastern spurs of the Mongolian Aerhtai Shan (Altai) and the eastern extremity of the Tian Shan. Its hills and low mountain ridges are dissected by ravines at its fringes. The Pendi Junggar runs southeast into the Trans-Aerhtai Shan Gobi, bounded by the Mongolian Aerhtai Shan and the Gobi Aerhtai Shan in the north and east, and the Altun Shan in the south. The basin can be further subdivided into two distinct portions. In the east, it is a sharp rugged plain broken by a mountainous spur that extends 6 miles (10 kilometers) into the plain. The western portion is a plain across which dry river beds meander; the plain's central part becomes increasingly fragmented by mesas and dry gullies.

The majority of rivers in the Gobi flow only when rains fall—mostly in the summer. Rivers that flow into the region from the surrounding mountains quickly disappear into the dry ground. The eastern

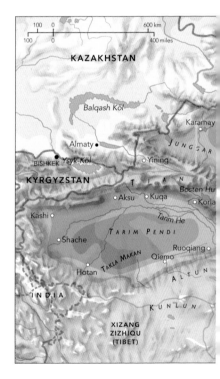

Deser — ▦ Desert
▦ Semiarid
Lakes
—— Rivers
♦ Mining/mineral exploration
• Oil and gas fields
—— Oil pipelines
● Capital cities
• Large cities
○ Other important towns/settlements
—— International boundaries

Mongolian Gobi region has more groundwater than the other parts of the desert. The water comes to the surface in small lakes and springs, but vegetation is still sparse. Other distinct regions of the Gobi include the Alashan Desert, which is bordered by the Qilian Shan range to the southwest and the Huang He River to the east. To the east of the Huang He lies the Mu Us (or Ordos) Desert.

Life in the Gobi

The vegetation of the Gobi consists mainly of salt-resistant plants. Species such as succulent grass (*Enchinochloa* spp.), tamarisk (*Tamarix* spp.) and stunted willow (*Salix* spp.), are sparsely distributed. In the semiarid regions, vegetation is slightly less sparse and does not need to be so hardy to survive; it includes such species as timuriya (*Timouria villosa*), and feather grass (*Stipa pennata*). Notable animals of the Gobi include Bactrian camels (*Camelus bactrianus*), ass kulans (*Equus asinus ferus*), the reintroduced Przewalski's wild horses (*Equus przewalskii*), gazelles (*Procapra* spp.), and ground squirrels.

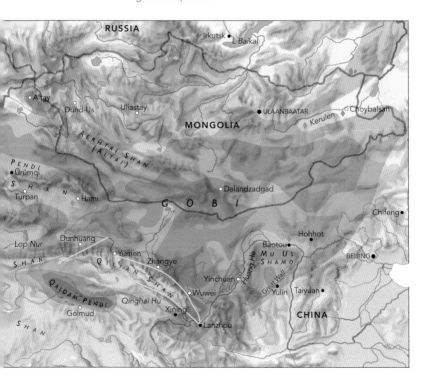

Peoples of the Gobi

The Mongolian language has 33 different words to describe the Gobi. These words classify types of terrain in terms of the vegetation that is growing there, and reflect not only the subtle diversity of the terrain, but also the close affinity that the peoples of the Gobi have with their inhospitable environment. Like most arid regions of the world, the Gobi is very sparsely populated.

The people of the Gobi Desert are predominantly Khalkha Mongols, who make up about 80 percent of the population of Mongolia. At the fringes of the Gobi, in the Inner Mongolian Autonomous Region of the People's Republic of China, Mongols are in a minority and ethnic Chinese compose the majority of the population.

The seminomadic pastoral lifestyle of the Khalkha Mongols has remained relatively unchanged for centuries. The main distinction between the Khalkha Mongols and other herdsmen in the region is that, because of the great harshness of their environment, they predominantly herd two-humped Bactrian camels. This species is better suited to the arid environment of the Gobi than is the horse, and is hardier than the one-humped Arabian camel (sometimes known as the dromedary). The 600,000 or so camels of the Gobi are not only essential for transporting the homes of the seminomads from pasture to pasture, but they are also sheared for their thick wool.

Although camels are numerous in the Gobi, sheep and goats are by far the most common livestock kept by the herdsmen. The sheep are particularly valuable as a source of meat, and the goats provide high-quality cashmere yarn. In the lusher semi-desert in the southwest of the region, herdsmen are also able to rear long-haired cattle.

Nomadic lifestyle

On average, nomadic herdsmen move about ten times a year. To make traveling easier, the herdsmen and their families live in lightweight structures, known as *ger*, which are made out of felt. Nomadism takes place on all scales, from short moves to fresh pasture, to longer seasonal migrations to escape the worst climatic extremes. The nomads of the Gobi usually live in family groups. The number of people in such groups is limited, and so this way of life helps to keep concentrations of people and livestock low in any particular area, thus not overstretching the desert's resources.

Where there is sufficient groundwater, as in the oases, some crops, such as melons and onions, are grown. However, the growing season is short and winter arrives early (in September) and is extremely harsh.

▼ *Several* gers *sit together on the sparse grassland steppeland of the Gobi Desert in Mongolia. The domed Mongol tents are often mistakenly called "yurts," but this terms refers to an accompanying open enclosure. The tent has a wooden framework and is covered with layers of hides and woven fabric, which are tied into place.*

Natural resources

The only oil ever discovered in the Gobi was around the town of Saynshand in the northeast of the region. The reserves were developed by the Chinese, and explorations have been carried out at deeper levels. However, the fact that the area has little water to support large populations, as well as being extremely isolated, could limit the economic viability of oil production. In some areas, salt and light metal ores are mined. Other products of the Gobi include scant quantities of coal, semiprecious stones, and aromatic woods.

Historically there were a fair number of cultivated oases in the Gobi, which provided rest points on caravan trails. These settlements generally flourished until their populations became too great for their water supply. Today, the main barrier to development is still the lack of water.

Mongolia as a whole has only recently begun to emerge from a period of prolonged economic stagnation and decline. There are a few small towns on the communication routes that cross the Gobi, such along the Beijing-Ulaanbaatar (Ulan Bator) railroad. In addition to this, there are regional administration centers, which provide basic services for the widely scattered herding populations. One such service is a boarding school system for the children of the herdsmen. The system allows the children a good level of education without it being disrupted by the nomadic lifestyle of the parents

Recently, the Chinese government has implemented programs in the southern parts of the desert to "reclaim the Gobi." Among these are projects experimenting with rice cultivation and viticulture. These are mostly at an experimental stage and are not economic in terms of returns on investment or in the use of the large amounts of scarce water needed. Other schemes include planting migrating sand dunes to prevent their continued advance on the fringes of the true steppeland of Inner Mongolia.

TIBET

Most of the high plateau of Tibet is desert. It is an autonomous region of China, located in the mountains of Asia. Covering an area about 470,000 square miles (1,200,000 square kilometers), the region is more than twice the size of France, and most of it lies above 15,000 feet (4,500 meters). Along the whole length of Tibet's southern borders lie the Himalayas. To the northwest lies the Kunlun Shan range, while to the northeast is the Tanggula Shan range.

The Tibetan plateau is a prime source of water for Central Asia, and groundwater and snow-melt feed the headwaters of the Indus, Brahmaputra, Salween, Mekong, Yangtze, and Huang He river systems. However, much of Tibet is desert, apart from the slightly lower and wetter southeastern fringes, and receives less than 10 inches (25 centimeters) of rain or snow each year. The low precipitation is due mainly to the Himalayas, which act as a barrier to the monsoon winds, bringing torrential rain to areas only 400 miles (640 kilometers) south of Tibet. In addition, violent winds sweep over much of Tibet all year round, and these have a desiccating effect. The high altitudes ensure that the temperatures over most of Tibet are cold. Tibet's climate is characterized by very long winters with extremely low nighttime temperatures, and short mild summers.

Surviving in the cold wilderness

Agriculture and pastoral nomadism are the two main activities. The waters of Tibet's major rivers are largely unavailable to the local population, who lack energy resources, manpower, or technology to transfer it to their fields. Instead, small groundwater-fed streams are tapped through systems of narrow channels and ponds, and led into terraced fields which are mainly situated on relatively level valley floors. The traditional staple crop in most of the area is barley, together with buckwheat, pulses and wheat, more recently potatoes, and in parts of the southeast, rice.

Between April and October, the animals (mainly cattle, yaks, sheep, and goats) are grazed on upland pastures. Their dairy produce is an essential ingredient of the local diet. The

▲ *A Tibetan yak herder* drives three yaks to upland pasture for summer grazing. In summer, the green valleys and mountains lend a tranquil air to the Tibetan scenery. In winter, however, low temperatures and icy winds can make venturing out of doors at all dangerous.

▨	Desert
▨	Semiarid
▨	Lakes
—	Rivers
•	Capital cities
•	Large cities
○	Other important towns/settlements
—	International boundaries

animals retained over the winter are accommodated in the lower stories of the farmhouses and fed on hay, clover, and other fodder. All the livestock, together with horses, mules, and donkeys, are also used as beasts of burden.

Since the 1950s, most Tibetan-populated areas have been subject to attempts to integrate them economically, culturally, and militarily with their neighbors. However, these attempts have been hampered by Tibet's remoteness and sparse population, as well as a cultural separateness based on its people's intense Buddhist faith. China has occupied Tibet since 1956, but has not succeeded in suppressing Tibetan cultural life. Projects for agricultural improvement have met with mixed success. A small local market and lack of surplus manpower make manufacturing uneconomic. A variety of minerals, including iron, manganese, magnesium, copper, lead, and zinc, has been found in Tibet. However, information on the precise amounts of mineral resources available is scarce. Tourism has been greatly developed since the 1970s, but is liable to political interruption.

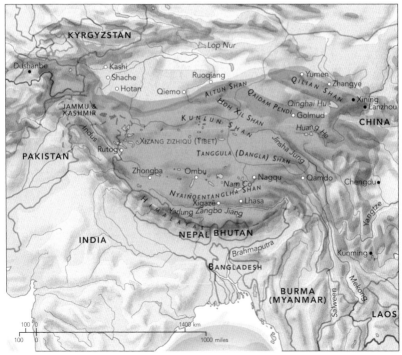

THE SONORAN AND CHIHUAHUAN DESERTS

The dry landscapes that dominate the entire southwestern quarter of North America are perhaps best conceived of as three fairly distinct desert cores. Each is surrounded by shrub and grass-covered transitions, and they are interrupted throughout by mountainous enclaves of woodland and forest. Some have called these "sky-islands" becaue they are islands of lush vegetation surrounded by a "sea" of desert. At the end of the Pleistocene, when aridity returned to these deserts, the flora and fauna of the sky islands were isolated, and some unique species and races have now evolved in them.

The Sonora Desert nearly encircles the Golfo de California (Gulf of California). It extends from sealevel northward into the lower valleys of California and Arizona, eastward into the Sierra foothills of Sonora, and in many places westward across the peninsula of Baja California to the shores of the Pacific. The Chihuahua Desert lies at a higher elevation (3,300–5,000 feet or 1,000–1,500 meters), and occupies the open northern end of Mexico's Mesa del Norte. It is flanked

▼ **Organ pipe,** cholla, and sanguaro cacti cover a hillside at Organ Pipe National Monument in Arizona.

Desert
Semiarid
Lakes
—— Rivers
♦ Mining/mineral exploration
○ Oil and gas fields
● Capital cities
• Large cities
○ Other important towns/settlements
—— International boundaries

to the east and west by zones of severely degraded grassland and woodland, which rise up to the Sierra and to the temperate Valley of Mexico on the Central Plateau.

Both Mexican deserts, in contrast to the Great Basin, which is described later, are essentially subtropical and are characterized by exceedingly rich floras containing annuals, woody perennials, and succulents, including many species of cactus. True barrenness is confined to dry lake beds or *playas* (salt flats and clay pans), rare tracts of mobile sand, "badlands" formed on deposits of shale and mudstone, and localized scree slopes and outcrops of rock.

163

Northern Mexico

Spanish exploitation of Mexico's dry north dates from the mid-16th century, scarcely two decades after the conquest of the Aztecs. The quest for land, silver, and souls to convert led quickly to the annihilation, assimilation, or displacement of nomadic bands of indigenous peoples who inhabited the area. The semiarid zones between the Sierras and the desert core contained the region's prized resources—minerals and rangeland—and provided the corridors for expansion. A few isolated outposts were founded far northward remarkably early, such as Santa Fe in 1609.

By the end of the 17th century, the frontier of settlement lay roughly along the current United States-Mexico border, and the essential characteristics of the rural economy and the landscape were well established. There were scattered mining centers and small agricultural settlements, but the grasslands were dominated by huge, unfenced, and virtually self-sufficient haciendas. These produced livestock—mostly cattle—for local consumption and for export to southern markets. The core deserts and rugged sierras were generally avoided, but provided a refuge for remnants of indigenous peoples, such as the Sari in coastal Sonora, and the Tarahumara in the mountains of western Chihuahua.

▼ **Aztec Ruins** National Monument in New Mexico is home to a number of structures and artefacts dating to around 1100 BCE. The site was once home to a group of Anasazi, who settled here to farm the fertile, irrigable soil. The area was abandoned in around 1300 due to climate change, increased population and shrinking natural resources.

With some notable exceptions, this pattern still persists. The United States is now the major market for Chihuahuan cattle, and copper production has outstripped that of silver. The revolution of 1910 brought a degree of land reform, and many of the large haciendas were dismantled. The Mexican Federal Government developed three important irrigated oases around the periphery of the Chihuahuan Desert—at points on the Rio Nazas and Rio Conchos, and along the lower Rio Bravo del Norte (the "Rio Grande" of Texas). Most of the winter lettuce and tomatoes consumed in the United States now come from irrigated fields on the coast of southern Sonora and northern Sinaloa, and Monterrey has become an important centre for steel production and a number of heavy manufacturing industries.

The US-Mexico border

The most striking changes have occurred along the United State-Mexico border. Tourism, based

▲ **Illegal immigration** *across the US-Mexican border has been a rising cause of concern in the southwest United States. Here US Border Patrol agents investigate a rudimentary tunnel starting near some abandoned customs buildings on the Mexican side, under the border between Tijuana and San Diego.*

initially on prostitution and the free availability of alcohol at a time when there were restrictive United States alcohol laws, accelerated rapidly during World War II at communities adjacent to United States military bases. A more broadly based tourist industry has since thrived at most significant crossing points. Since initiation in 1965, the Border Industries Program, which takes advantage of United States' tax laws and low Mexican wages, has attracted more than 1,000 *maquiladora* factories, or assembly plants (largely American-owned), and 250,000 workers (entirely Mexican) to rapidly growing border communities. There are now a dozen major "twin" United States-Mexico settlements clustered along the international boundary. More recently, the huge illegal immigration from Mexico into the United States, on which much of US agriculture depends, has become a political issue in the United States. Fences and walls are appearing along the line of the border in a vain attempt to control the flow.

THE GREAT BASIN

The largest of the deserts in the United States lie between the Rocky Mountains and the wall of mountains from the Sierra Nevada of California through to the Cascades Range of Oregon and Washington. The region is a mid-latitude rain-shadow desert, cool, even cold in winter and blistering hot in summer.

Mountain and basin

The Great Basin is not a single depression, but in fact a collection of basins, and is the area from which the term "mountain-and-basin," to describe the endless stretches of alternating mountain ranges and desert flats, originates. A series of upfaulted mountain blocks separates another series of basins. The ranges in the Great Basin are generally aligned north-south and are typically 60 miles (100 kilometers) or more in length. The upper slopes are frequently covered with pine and juniper stands, or occasionally with fragrant pine forest. The zone between mountain base and basin floor is known as the "piedmont" and is made up of eroded material carried by streams, and spread out in great fans from where the rivers valley spill into the basins. Piedmont zones comprise about 70 percent of the Great Basin and contain its cover of shrubs, dominated in most places by greasewood, sage brush (*Artemisia* spp.), and saltbush (*Atriplex* spp.). The basins themselves are filled with lake sediment, some of it saline. In some of the basins, there are shorelines of huge lakes that were filled at the time of the last glaciation—Lake Bonneville being the best known and biggest. Its shorelines are clearly visible from the train or the great highways that now traverse the basins.

Death Valley National Monument is the deepest of these basins, reaching down to below sealevel.

The plateaux

The Colorado Plateau is a wedge-shaped area of about 125,000 square miles (325,000 square kilometers) between the southern parts of the Rockies and Great Basin, extending south into Arizona and New Mexico. Its geology and landforms are strikingly different from neighboring areas. The region is underlain throughout by massive, ancient beds of marine and aeolian sandstones, shales and limestones that have been deformed, uplifted, and deeply incised by the Colorado River and its tributaries. This is a land of extensive plateaus and flat-topped mesas (steep-sided tablelands). Colorful orange and red rocks are exposed in abundant cliffs and spectacular canyons, including the Grand Canyon itself.

Desert
Semiarid
Lakes
— Rivers
♦ Mining/mineral exploration
· Oil and gas fields
● Capital cities
● Large cities
○ Other important towns/settlements
— International boundaries

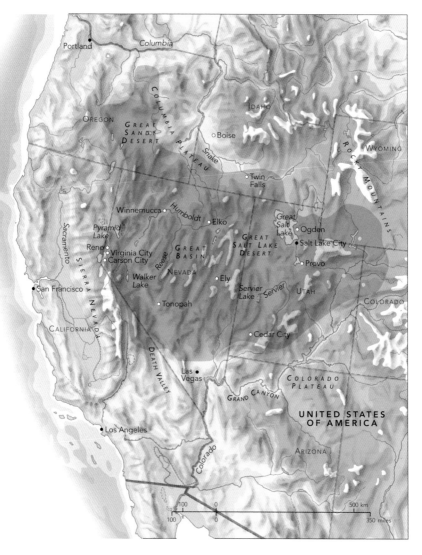

The Columbia Plateau is a dry tableland covering some 50,000 square miles (130,000 square kilometers) of eastern Oregon and Washington, and the Snake River Plain of southern Idaho. It is covered with layers of solidified lava, which are 6,600 feet (2,000 meters) thick in places. The Columbia River and its major tributaries have carved canyons through parts of the plateau, forming ideal sites for dams.

A modern wilderness

The first European settlers to arrive in the intermontane deserts were miners and Mormon colonists. These two contrasting groups soon displaced the indigenous, nomadic population, which included tribes of the Navajo, Shoshone, and Ute.

Following the California Gold Rush of 1849–59, a wave of prospectors moved eastward, combing the Great Basin and Rocky Mountains for signs of gold and silver. Numerous strikes gave rise to flourishing mining towns, but most of these communities were shortlived. In Nevada, still known as the Silver State, the scars and debris of past abandoned mining activities are widespread. A few sizable "ghost towns," such as Virginia City, have escaped fire and vandalism to become significant tourist attractions. Mining and processing of gold, silver, copper, and other metallic ores are important in isolated localities today, but their regional economic significance is dwarfed by gambling, tourism and manufacturing.

Mormon colonies

The Mormons—members of the Church of Jesus Christ of the Latter-Day Saints—arrived at the site of Salt Lake City in 1847. After the first years of hardship in the unfamiliar desert environment, the sect rapidly evolved social institutions, agricultural practices, and colonial policies, which proved remarkably effective for the expansion of their empire throughout the intermontane West. Wherever supplies of water could be developed, small groups of families were dispatched to establish villages. Green fields, orchards, and pastures were sustained by irrigation, and surrounding deserts and woodlands served as common rangelands.

▼ *Two satellite images* show the rapid expansion of Las Vegas between 1973 and 2000. The "greening" of the city's fast-growing suburbs costs 190 gallons (870 liters) of water per person per day, with 70% of residential water being used for outdoor activities, such as watering lawns and washing cars. It is feared that unless alternative sources of water are found, the town will run dry in about 50 years. This has led to clashes between the city's authorities and local farmers, in what has become to be known as the "craps versus crops" debate.

▲ **Monument Valley,** *Arizona, is one of the most famous desert landscapes in the world, thanks to its appearance in numerous Westerns. Although the towering buttes and rock pillars are especially spectacular, the barren rocky landscape is typical of that crossed by the early miners and settlers of the mid-19th century.*

Some of the villages have been urbanized and lost their original character, notably Salt Lake City and Las Vegas. Many experienced growth and change as they acquired additional functions in government, tourism, forestry, manufacturing, and mining. Scores of Mormon settlements were abandoned, especially in parts of southern Utah, as rangelands deteriorated and irrigation systems were eroded.

The public domain

Federally owned land—the so-called Public Domain—is especially prominent in the dry intermontane West, where it comprises 86 percent of the state of Nevada and 66 percent of Utah. Federal stewardship has profoundly influenced the use and conservation of these areas, with initially disastrous consequences. There were only minimal restrictions on use and there was a popular notion that any individual had rights to publicly held resources. This encouraged the removal of forests, indiscriminate slaughter of wildlife, and the stocking of ranges far beyond their sustainable capacities. As a result of such exploitation, many areas had reached the peak of economic and ecological productivity before the end of the 19th century and have declined ever since.

Changes in public attitude and government policy have come slowly, but are now incorporated in hundreds of laws that carve the Public Domain into various types of management units with unique objectives for utilization, preservation, and reclamation.

169

The deserts of southeastern California are generally divided into two regions. The southern part, which lies at lower altitude, is really an extension of the Sonora Desert and is often called the Colorado Desert or simply the "Low Desert." The Sonora Desert covers much of southwest Arizona and northwest Mexico. The higher altitudes to the north of the Sonora, dominated by extensive stands of creosote bush (*Larrea tridentate*), are known to known to Californians as the Mojave Desert or "High Desert."

The Colorado River

Today, hardly a drop of water passes through the lower reaches of the Colorado River unless a valve is opened. The river that carved the Grand Canyon once had the power—during an extended flood 90 years ago—to escape through a small irrigation canal and create California's Salton Sea. But today, its waters are used, reused, and exported hundreds of miles to the major urban centers of Arizona and California. The keystone of confinement was the Hoover Dam (completed in 1936), which created Lake Mead. This was followed shortly by the Parker Dam (1938) with its reservoir, Lake Havasu, which is the source of the great Colorado River Aqueduct and the more recent Granite Reef Aqueduct conveying water to central Arizona. A series of smaller dams was constructed downstream to irrigate lands along the lower Colorado and to divert water to oases in the Imperial Valley and along the lower Gila River. The Davis Dam (1954) eased regulation and increased storage capacity. The last dam, Glen Canyon (1966), was built to slow siltation in Lake Mead. The Colorado system controls floods, generates sizable amounts of electricity, provides irrigation and municipal supplies of water and supports an important recreation industry. Ecologically, however, control of the river has been a disaster, altering river bank habitats along the lower valley and through the Grand Canyon. The proposed Bridge Canyon Dam would have backed water into the middle reaches of the Grand Canyon, but economic considerations and environmental groups halted the project.

Vegetation change

Since the mid-19th century, there have been significant vegetation changes in the Sonora Desert of southern Arizona. In some places, habitats have been obliterated, exotic species have been introduced and the mix and composition of

▼ *A satellite image* of Death Valley, California. Flanked by mountains, Death Valley is the lowest place in the United States. Altogether some 560 sq mi (1,400 km²) of the valley floor lie below sea-level. Through the peculiarities of California's physical geography and climate, Death Valley lies only about 75 mi (125 km) from Sequoia National Park, which contains some of the world's largest trees.

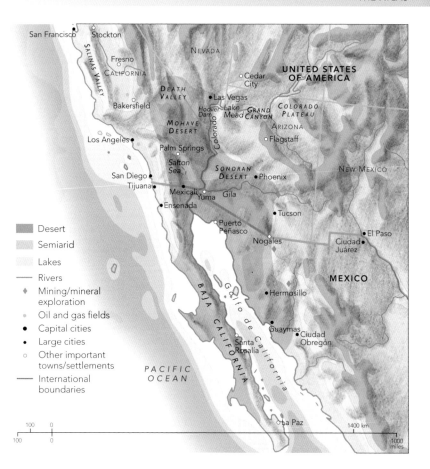

Desert
Semiarid
Lakes
— Rivers
♦ Mining/mineral exploration
○ Oil and gas fields
● Capital cities
● Large cities
○ Other important towns/settlements
— International boundaries

native species has been altered. Efforts to preserve vanishing river bank zones—especially groves of cottonwood (*Populus fremontii*) and willow (*Salix* sp.), and wet marshes—have been a major focus for local conservation groups.

The deterioration of the grasslands became apparent in the 1880s, soon after the large-scale introduction of cattle. Grass cover was greatly reduced and more than 20 plant species were introduced. Perhaps one-half of the 9,000,000 acres (3,600,000 hectares) of "mesquite land" in Arizona has appeared since about 1860. However, these changes are complex and are not necessarily negative. Many ranges throughout the western United States are today in far better condition than during peak periods of heavy grazing, which typically occurred before 1990.

The Sun Belt

The state of California uses an annual total of 47 million acre feet (58 billion cubic meters) of fresh water. Around half of this is pumped from groundwater reserves, principally in the Central Valley. The surface supply comes mainly from the western slopes of the Sierra Nevada where there are numerous reservoirs supplying a maze of canals that lead to croplands in the Central Valley. A smaller amount derives from the dry eastern slopes of the Sierras, mainly to the benefit of southern California. In most years, the Colorado River has contributed a far greater share to the total supply than California's legal allotment of 4 million acre feet (5 billion cubic meters) would suggest. As Arizona begins to utilize its share more fully, California's use will decline.

Huge amounts of water are transferred throughout the state, generally from the wet northern region to the dry southern region. The most spectacular transfers involve three great aqueducts that converge on the Los Angeles Basin: the Colorado River Aqueduct, the Los Angeles Aqueduct from the eastern slopes of the Sierra Nevada, and the California Aqueduct from the "Delta" region of the Central Valley near Stockton. The aqueduct from the Sierra Nevada to San Francisco is also impressive, as is the All American Canal that feeds Colorado River water to the Imperial Valley.

Depleted groundwater

About 82 percent of the total supply, including both groundwater and surface water, is used to irrigate crops. Roughly 85 percent of the state's 15,000 square miles (40,000 square kilometers) of irrigated cropland is in the Central Valley, but there are other important areas: the Imperial Valley and Paolo Verde Valley along the lower Colorado River, both of which lie in the Low Desert; and the Salinas Valley and Oxnard Plain, which lie between Los Angeles and San Francisco in moderately humid coastal locations. Several valleys near Los Angeles continued to produce irrigated crops until they were displaced by urban growth during the 1960s. Supplies of groundwater were once abundant in the deep sediments of the Los Angeles Basin and other coastal valleys. However, these have been seriously depleted by a century of crop production and urban growth to the point where salt water is now spreading into aquifers along the coastal margins of the basin. To halt the intrusion of salt water, a chain of injection wells has been established, which create a barrier of fresh water. During periods when reservoirs along the Colorado are full, "excess" water is imported to the coastal margins in an attempt to recharge aquifers.

The Navajo Reservation

More than 90,000 Native Americans live on Arizona's share of the Navajo Reservation, which also includes adjacent strips of New Mexico, Colorado and Utah. This "Four Corners" section of the Colorado Plateau is well known for its scenery and archaeological interest. But it is also the home of the Navajo. Herds of sheep and goats graze on tufts of grass amongst the sage. Scattered across the ranges are isolated clusters of dwellings, including the ubiquitous *hogans* (the earth-covered, wooden structures typical of the Navajo). Pickup trucks or horse-drawn "buckboards" are used for transport, although there is the occasional lone rider on horseback. Small settlements are built around the essential and often crowded trading post. In the larger towns, identical prefabricated homes focus around the water tower, school, hospital, or administrative building. There are alarming levels of unemployment and many signs of rural poverty. Arizona alone has 23 nominally sovereign reservations, which incorporate 30,000 square miles (80,000 square kilometers) of land, and house about 80 percent of the state's 200,000 Native Americans.

▼ **A satellite image** of Phoenix, Arizona. Phoenix, the state capital of Arizona, is a modern version of the traditional oasis city, where trees, lawns, and swimming pools all thumb their noses at the arid desert climate. The water that supplies Phoenix comes from the Roosevelt Dam (completed 1911) on the Salt River, about 60 mi (100 km) to the northeast of the city.

COASTAL CHILE AND PERU

The Pacific coast owes its aridity to the Humboldt Current, which brings cold water from the Antarctic, cooling the surface of the ocean and producing fog and stratus clouds, but almost no rain. The Atacama Desert of Chile and the Sechura Desert of Peru are both hyperarid. In the Peruvian desert, direct contact with the sea produces a cloudy climate, with nocturnal fogs. The coastal influence declines rapidly inland to ranges of snowcapped mountains and intervening basins.

Basins and pans

The Atacama, between Arica and Vallenar, occupies two longitudinal belts: the Intermontane Longitudinal Depression and the Coastal Cordillera (or Tange); but from Chañaral to the southern limit, it is developed in transverse basins. The Intermontane Longitudinal Depression is divided into three parts: between Arica and Quebrada de Tana it is a plain, or piedmont, of sediments accumulated at the foot of the Andes. Near the Coastal Range, these sediments collect in *playas* (with saline deposits). The valley is deeply incised by valleys known as *quebradas*, whose rivers drain into the sea, but are very intermittent. From Quebrada de Tana to the Loa River, the depression is closed and contains the Pampa del Tamarugal. Finally, between the Loa River and the basin of Chañaral, there are well-defined basins without runoff of water, but open to the sea, in which there are saline depressions known as *salars*. A typical feature of the contact between the inner foot of the Coastal Range and the Longitudinal Depression is the veneer of sodium nitrate, whose origin is still mysterious.

Desert climate

There are two types of climate in the Atacama. The narrow coastal belt has nearly 110 cloudy days in the year, mainly in winter. Stratus clouds and fogs known as *camanchacas* are typical. Nevertheless, the lack of rainfall is almost absolute, and rain comes only from sporadic, severe storms, often many years apart. The fogs

▼ *A satellite image* of the Atacama Desert, northern Chile. Here salt pans and gorges choked with mineral-streaked sediments give way to white-capped volcanoes. Much of the Atacama Desert occupies a series of high basins, or troughs, located between barren peaks. In these inhospitable inland regions, the average elevation of the desert landscape is in excess of 6,500 ft (2,000 m).

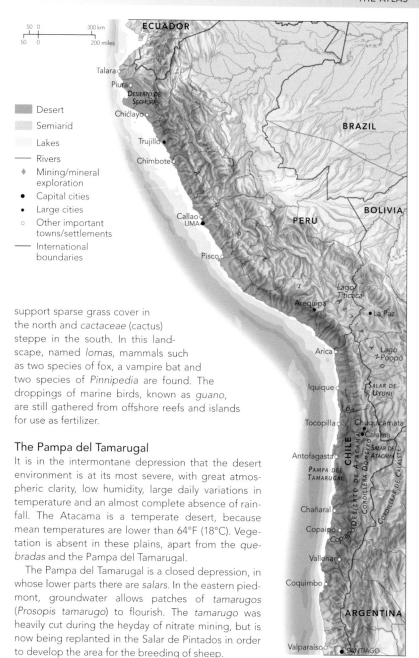

Desert

Semiarid

Lakes

— Rivers

♦ Mining/mineral exploration

• Capital cities

• Large cities

○ Other important towns/settlements

— International boundaries

support sparse grass cover in the north and *cactaceae* (cactus) steppe in the south. In this land-scape, named *lomas*, mammals such as two species of fox, a vampire bat and two species of *Pinnipedia* are found. The droppings of marine birds, known as *guano*, are still gathered from offshore reefs and islands for use as fertilizer.

The Pampa del Tamarugal

It is in the intermontane depression that the desert environment is at its most severe, with great atmospheric clarity, low humidity, large daily variations in temperature and an almost complete absence of rainfall. The Atacama is a temperate desert, because mean temperatures are lower than 64°F (18°C). Vegetation is absent in these plains, apart from the *quebradas* and the Pampa del Tamarugal.

The Pampa del Tamarugal is a closed depression, in whose lower parts there are *salars*. In the eastern piedmont, groundwater allows patches of *tamarugos* (*Prosopis tamarugo*) to flourish. The *tamarugo* was heavily cut during the heyday of nitrate mining, but is now being replanted in the Salar de Pintados in order to develop the area for the breeding of sheep.

Development of the Atacama

Human settlement and agriculture in the Atacama have been possible only around four groups of oases: Arica near the Peruvian border, the eastern edge of the Pampa del Tamarugal, and the basins of the Loa and Copiapó rivers. When the Spanish arrived, they found that the valley bottoms, or *quebradas*, in the longitudinal depression between Arica and Quebrada de Tana were extraordinarily fertile. The chronicler Cristóbal de Molina described the area's "beautiful farmlands" and irrigation systems. According to the natives, it never rained, but the area never lacked water. In each valley springs allowed them to irrigate their fields and vegetable gardens. Today, irrigation in this region is possible only by means of wells, whose water is generally slightly saline. In modern times, the principal crops are corn and alfalfa.

For the villages along the eastern edge of the Pampa del Tamarugal, irrigation is made possible by traditional subterranean conduits similar to the *foggara* of the Sahara. In the central Atacama, the Loa River—whose source lies high in the Andes—has been used to irrigate alfalfa. The Loa takes water to Calama, the ancient centre for the production of nitrates as well as the modern center of Chile's copper industry. Alfalfa is also grown in the valley of the Copiapó River and in the Vallenar Basin in the Norte Chico semidesert. In the Copiapó valley in particular, agricultural modernization has produced major changes since the 1980s. These include new patterns of land use, the expansion of land under cultivation, and the increasing production of fruit.

Mining the Atacama

Following the discovery of silver by Spanish pioneer Juan Godoy near Copiapó in 1832, mines were opened up in the Atacama. However, until the construction of a railroad between Copiapó and Caldera Bay—the first railroad in the southern hemisphere—exports were limited by the capacity of mule trains. Later, silver was discovered near Chañarcillo, and the population of the Copiapó valley grew spectacularly.

Despite the silver rush of the 19th century, mineral exploitation of the Atacama dates back to pre-Columbian times, when farmers along the eastern border of the Pampa del Tamarugal extracted *caliche*, a salt deposit containing sodium nitrate (saltpeter), used in the manufacture of fertilizer. After the arrival of the Spanish, the crushing and leaching of *caliche* flourished as a home industry.

During the 19th century, the Chilean nitrates were heavily exploited following the exhaustion of the guano deposits

▲ **The Chuquicamata** copper mine, near Calama in the Atacama Desert, Chile, is the world's largest copper mine in both size and levels of production. Although most desert environments are still relatively free of industrial pollution, the presence of heavy industry has had a damaging effect on parts of the Atacama. Huge amounts of dust are created by the open-cast mining techniques used for extracting the copper ore.

along the coast and on many offshore islands. The nitrate industry boomed toward the end of the century. Rail construction made possible the development of several centers of production. At the industry's height, 150 factories were in operation. But after the German invention of synthetic nitrates during World War I, the Chilean nitrate industry suffered severely, and the landscape of the nitrate *pampas* began to change. Only a few factories are active today, and decayed remnants of towns, villages, and railroads still dot the desert. Nevertheless, present production still provides nitrate, iodine, borax, and sodium sulphate, which are used for various purposes.

The mining of copper

Copper mining in the Atacama dates from the 1700s. With the decline of nitrate mining, copper increased in importance. On the western ridge of the Andean Cordillera, ancient volcanic activity and seismic movements produced mineral-bearing strata, including the world's largest concentration of copper ore. The largest mines were established after 1915, mainly near the Loa River and Potrerillos, in the Chañaral basin. At Chuquicamata, terraces have been blasted ever downward, so that the mine is now some 1,900 feet (580 meters) below the surface of the desert.

From 1938 to 1975, over 220 million tons of spoil from the Potrerillos and El Salvador copper mines were dumped on the coast, in Chañaral Bay, causing dramatic changes in the beach, which advanced at a rate of some 80 feet (25 meters) each year. The contaminated area extends for 10 miles (16 kilometers) along the shore, and the beaches now have a high content of spoil. A dramatic drop in biological diversity in the area seems to be associated with copper in the sediments and pollutants in the water.

VENEZUELA GUYANA

COLOMBIA

SURINAME FRENCH GUIANA

QUITO

Ambato

ECUADOR

Guayaquil

Cuenca

A M A Z O N

Amazonas

B A S I N

Chiclayo

Trujillo

Chimbote

Huánuco

PERÚ

Huancayo

LIMA

BRAZIL

Cuzco

Lago Titicaca

BOLIVIA

M A T O G R O S S O D O S U L

Arequipa

LA PAZ

Oruro

Santa Cruz

Arica

Sucre

SALAR DE UYUNI

PACIFIC

OCEAN

SALAR DE ATACAMA

PARAGUAY

Antofagasta

San Miguel De Tucumán

La Roja

Santiago del Estero

ATLANTIC

OCEAN

Valparaíso

San Juan

Córdoba

SANTIAGO

Mendoza

Rosario

San Rafael

URUGUAY

ARGENTINA

Montevideo

BUENOS AIRES

Concepción

Santa Rosa

Neuquén

Bahía Blanca

Valdivia

Negro

Puerto Montt

Sierra Grande

Chubut

Rawson

Comodoro Rivadavia

Puerto Deseado

PATAGONIA

Río Gallegos

Punta Arenas

CHILE

GRAN CHACO

PANTANAL

100 0   1400 km

100 0   1000 miles

NORTH
ATLANTIC
OCEAN

• Foraleza
○ Natal
• Recife
☆
•• Salvador

SOUTH
ATLANTIC
OCEAN

Desert
Semiarid
Lakes
—— Rivers
♦ Mining/mineral
   exploration
○ Oil and gas fields
—— Oil pipelines
● Capital cities
● Large cities
○ Other important
   towns/settlements
—— International
   boundaries

In southern Peru, the Andes Mountains divide into two major prongs: the Cordillera Occidental and the Cordillera Central. These high ranges enclose the desert of the Altiplano (high plains), which lies mainly within the borders of Bolivia. The Altiplano is a closed depression, 11,500–13,000 feet (3,500–4,000 meters) above sea level. It is filled by eroded sediments and volcanic material. The region is characterized by, among other things, vast flat *salars* (salt basins), which are the remnants of ancient lakes.

In Chile, the Codillera de Domeyko—an offshoot of the Cordillera Occidental—encloses the huge Salar de Atacama in an intermontane depression. The basin is filled with sediments, and a broad, elonged *salar* at 7,550–7,850 feet (2,300–2,400 meters) above sea-level. In the oases along the eastern edge of this basin, farmers raise crops, irrigated by ancient systems, and livestock.

South of the Bolivian Altiplano, northern Argentina contains a number of inward-draining depressions. The principal of these depressions contain *salars*. The southern end of the Andean desert is where the Cordillera Central and Cordillera Occidental converge.

Climate, flora, and fauna

Climatic conditions on the Altiplano are marked by strong and persistent winds and great daily temperature variations. In the Bolivian section, annual rainfall averages some 8 inches (200 millimeters), with no marked seasonal variations. However, rainfall drops significantly from west to east. Visitors to these high regions almost invariably suffer from altitude sickness.

At an altitude of around 11,500–13,000 feet (3,500–4,000 meters), the vegetation consists mainly of small shrubs. The dominant species is utola (*Baccharis tola*). On the western slopes of the Cordillera Occidental, the principal plants are various species of Cactaceae (cacti and their relatives.) On the slopes of the *salars* in the Puna, the gramineous (grassy) species known as pajonal dominates. In the basin of the Salar de Atacama, slightly higher rainfall allows the development of some denser plant communities. The chief species is the cachiyuyo (*Acantholippia atacamensis*), which is consumed by cattle in the oases. The lower slopes of volcanoes bordering the basins of the Altiplano are home to llareta plants (*Azorella compacta*), which are used for fuel.

The semidesert of Patagonia

In the southern Argentinian provinces of Chubut and Santa Cruz, arid tablelands dominate the landscape from sealevel to about 3,300 feet (1,000 meters). Because the prevailing

179

▲ **Located in the** southeastern Argentinian province of Chubut, the Valdés Peninsula features arid tablelands that rise steeply from the sea, reaching a height of about 3,300 ft (1,000 m).

westerly winds lose their moisture while crossing the southern stretches of the Andes, Patagonia is a cold semi-desert in which precipitation falls principally in winter. Temperatures average only 45°F (7°C) throughout the year, and the many days of frost and snow, and persistent westerly winds restrict the vegetation cover considerably. In closed depressions known locally as *bajos*, the accumulation of dust and salts produce *salitrales* (salt pans).

Plateaux and plains

Before the Spanish Conquest, Lake Titicaca in the Altiplano was holy to the Incas. The Spanish began to occupy the Altiplano in the late 1530s, and the conquest was more or less complete by 1600. The Spanish presence in the Altiplano has never been large, however, when compared to other areas of South America. As a result, a large part of the population is still purely or largely of aboriginal descent.

There are few resources to exploit. Exceptions are the very fine wool taken from vicuña and guanaco skins. The animals are hunted in the high grassland areas. Vicuña in particular have come under severe threat from hunting, largely because their very fine wool is highly prized (it is said to be twice as fine as sheep's wool). Already in the late 1960s, the population was estimated to be below 10,000. But a number of initiatives are helping to halt the decline. First, in Peru, the vicuña are now the legal property of local people (in the hope that this would encourage better management of the valuable resource. The result is a rapid resuscitation of the vicuña population (although there are still problems of managing the grazing of the range).

Mining the Altiplano

The Spanish began to exploit the mineral wealth of the Altiplano region in the 16th century. The city of Potosí, for example, started to grow rapidly when silver was discovered in 1545. Tin mining started to become economically important toward the end of the 19th century.

The tin is usually found in the same regions of the Altiplano as silver, in a belt that runs from north to south through the Cordillera Real. Both tin and silver are still mined in large quantities. There are also mines producing smaller amounts of copper, lead, antimony, tungsten, and zinc.

There is severe local environmental damage caused by mining, particularly large open-cast pits. Economic problems arising from falling world commodity prices may not directly increase such problems, but serve to prevent many clean-up and damage-limitation operations that might have been undertaken.

Farming and mining in Patagonia

Until the late 19th century, Patagonia was inhabited by only a few, widely dispersed Indians, most of whom lived by hunting. In the 1880s, Argentine troops undertook a campaign that gained control of the region. Few descendants of the original inhabitants remain, and there has been no very large immigration of Europeans. After gaining control of the region, the Argentine government decided to give away large blocks of land, and most of these are now run on the *estancia* ranching system. Most agriculture consists of livestock rearing in the vast dry areas, although some irrigated parts, such as the upper Negro Valley, grow a wide variety of fruit and some vegetable produce. Because of the harsh environment, the shelter provided by valleys is as important as a supply of water.

Minerals extracted include coal, gas, and oil, the latter two being produced particularly in the Comodoro Rivadavia region. There are significant deposits of iron ore in Sierra Grande, but only small amounts of other minerals, including uranium, lead, and zinc.

Large hydroelectric schemes have been built on the upper branches of the Rio Negro. These schemes seem to have caused no severe ecological damage other than the flooding of quite large areas of the desert. More schemes are planned, however, and it is hard to tell what the effects might be.

The main ecological problem arising from human activity is the destruction of vegetation by the more or less uncontrolled grazing of animals. The increased soil erosion that this causes has led to considerable expansion of desert areas.

▼ *An Argentinian cowboy (gaucho) on a cattle drive in Patagonia. Cattle rearing is possible in the harsh Patagonian environment thanks largely to the numerous valleys that protect both the cattle and the drivers from strong winds.*

DESERTS OF AUSTRALIA

Australia has few totally barren deserts, and yet, except for Antarctica, it is the continent with the greatest area of desert. This apparent paradox results from the fact that a few thousand years ago Australia was more arid than it is today and has inherited many desert-like landforms. In addition, rainfall is so unreliable that areas in the semiarid zone may appear very arid at times. However, overall there is sufficient rain for the survival of hardy vegetation.

In Australia, the arid zone lies between the 10-inch (250-millimeter) isohyet (a line drawn through areas that share the same amount of rainfall) in the south, and the 20-inch (500-millimeter) isohyet in the north. The Australian climate is notable for great variability from year to year.

- Desert
- Semiarid
- Lakes
- — Rivers
- ♦ Mining/mineral exploration
- Oil and gas fields
- ● Capital cities
- ● Large cities
- ○ Other important towns/settlements
- — International boundaries

Geological history
When the ancient supercontinent of Gondwana broke up, the final split between Australia and Antarctica occurred about 55 million years ago. Antarctica has hardly moved since

▶ **Pinnacles Desert,**
Western Australia,
comprises thousands
of limestone pillars,
some of which stand
16 ft (5 m) high. The
pinnacles were formerly
lime-rich sand dunes
formed from sand blown
inland from the coast.

then, whereas Australia has drifted north. The continent did not drift from a cold climate to a warm one, but was warm and wet until it reached its present position. Drying started a few million years ago, but the exceptionally arid conditions of modern-day Australia started less than one million years ago. Although one million years is a short period in geological timescale, the dry conditions have existed long enough for biological adaptations to emerge

Desert types

Australia's deserts can be divided into three main types; clay plain deserts, sandy deserts, and stony deserts. Clay plain deserts are fundamentally alluvial plains formed when rivers deposit clay and silt. Sandy deserts are characterized in the main by remarkably parallel linear dunes, although there are small areas with other dune patterns. The Simpson Desert, an example of this type, has exceptionally long and straight dunes, between which lie clay swales (moist depressions). Sandy deserts with lakes may also have lunettes, crescent-shaped dunes on the downwind side of lakes.

Stony deserts can be subdivided into four smaller categories—shield deserts, range and valley deserts, limestone deserts, and gibber plains. Shield deserts, sitting on the Precambrian shield, an area of ancient granite and metamorphic rocks, dominate Western Australia. Much of this shield is deeply weathered and has a long landscaping history.

Range and valley deserts are deserts that lie on folded strata, while limestone deserts, such as Nullarbor Plain, lie on horizontal limestone. Gibber plains are stony (another word for gibber is desert pavement) that overlie fairly stone-free soil.

Much of the drainage of inland Australia is internal, and surface runoff is unreliable. Groundwater is often saline, but in some situations a thin layer of fresh water lies on top.

183

Sandy desert

Stony desert

Clay plain desert

▲ **Australia's deserts** *can be broadly categorized into three main types: sandy, stony, and clay plain.*

This layer is important for a number of species of plants and animals.

Australia's desert lakes range from very small to vast. The largest is Lake Eyre, which lies about 40 feet (12 meters) below sea-level and has an area of 3,600 square miles (9,300 square kilometers). Lake Eyre has been flooded 20 times in the last 40 years; there were large floods in 1950, 1974, and 1984. After the 1950 flood, which virtually filled the basin, the lake took two years to dry out.

People in desert Australia

People have survived in the Australian arid zone for many thousands of years. The earliest human remains are about 40,000 year old and belong to ancestors of the Australian Aborigines. Occupation sites, however, have been discovered dating back 60,000 years, and biological evidence suggests that people may well have arrived even earlier—about 140,000 years ago.

When European settlement began in 1788 the numbers of Aborigines declined very quickly, especially in the fertile margins of the country. The Europeans grouped them together and placed them in missions and reserves. Although they now have their own tribal lands, many have moved into the towns. In recent years, however, there has been an "outstation" movement, with small groups of Aboriginals moving to remote settlements, where they can live in a more traditional manner in the desert.

Aboriginal hunter-gatherers are generally perceived as living in harmony with their environment. Recently, some scientists have suggested that their hunting affected the local animal populations, and that larger animals may have been killed off. There is also some evidence that the early people changed their environment very radically by fire. It has also been suggested that Aboriginal gathering of plants for food affected the Australian ecology.

The European invasion

Whether Aboriginal hunting-gathering techniques damaged the environment or not, there is little doubt about the effect Europeans had on the arid and semiarid lands. The consequences of clearing, overgrazing, and overcultivating were devastating. Massive clearing projects were undertaken to make way for the pastoralists. They would move into the arid lands during a "good" time, when the rains were heavy, but then withdraw when the land once again became too arid, leaving a barren wasteland behind them.

▲ *Three Australian Aborigines play traditional instruments, with the man on the right playing the didgeridoo, perhaps the best known instrument. Most Aboriginal songs serve a traditional ceremonial purpose, and have been passed down for generations.*

Clearing forest and bush was done for several reasons other than making the ground available for grazing. In the Kalgoorlie region, for example, treestumps show that this "arid" area was forested at the time of the first gold rush in the late 19th century. The trees were destroyed in vast numbers for building and for smelting gold.

On marginal lands, the extreme technique of "recreational plowing" is practiced. If good rains follow, a crop is achieved; if the rain, however, is insufficient, the farmers still collect a subsidy. Such practices contribute greatly to the problem of erosion. As a result, dust storms have been known to carry "red rain" from the topsoil of the arid zone as far as Melbourne.

Livestock management

Compounding the problem of erosion, many cattle and sheep are now reared in the arid lands. Their numbers often exceed the carrying capacity of the land, leading to severe erosion. In western New South Wales, 15 million sheep grazed on the arid lands before the drought of the 1890s, when the number was reduced to 3 million, returning later to 7 million. Many people believe that trampling by hoofed animals was particularly destructive in Australia, where the native animals have soft feet.

Introduced animals also compete with the native fauna for food and water. This applies not only to domestic animals, but also to their feral equivalents (wild horses, camels, buffalo, dogs), and to the rabbit and its introduced predator, the fox. Introduced plants also change the ecology. Buffel grass,

185

for example, was introduced to conserve soil and halt erosion. However, it is inedible to most indigenous animals.

A modern form of land use in the desert is tourism. A few places have become major attractions, and Uluru (Ayers Rock) now has over 250,000 visitors per year. Such numbers require considerable development of roads, water supplies waste disposal and accommodation, all of which have a marked effect on the environment.

Water and mining
Because surface water is scarce in Australia, groundwater or imported water is used. Much of eastern Australia lies on the Great Artesian Basin, a vast, basin-shaped aquifer that has an area of some 6.5 million square miles (17 million square kilometers), about 20 percent of Australia. The Great Artesian Basin leaks naturally in a few areas, but there are about 18,000 boreholes tapping the resource. Much of the water is suitable for watering stock, but too saline for irrigation. Now that the water can be deleted, it is known that much of it is very ancient "fossil" water, which is not being renewed (although there is some renewal from wetter parts of the continent).

Watering schemes
Some towns are maintained by piped water. Kalgoorlie in Western Australia, for example, was supplied by the Goldfields Water Scheme, which was completed in 1903. The scheme consisted of a 320-mile (520-kilometer) pipeline conveying over 4.4 million gallons (20 million liters) per day. This has since been extended to the Goldfields and Agricultural Water Scheme that now serves 12,000 square miles (30,000 square kilometers) of farmland.

Australia has both active irrigation schemes and the rather more fanciful "engineer's dreams." The economics of irrigation have been severely attacked, but the practice continues. Its worst consequence is salinization.

The best known of the so-called "engineer's dreams" was the Bradfield scheme of the 1930s, whereby the Tully, Herbert, and Burdekin rivers were to be diverted into an inland irrigation area. Another scheme was to flood Lake Torrens in South Australia with seawater and so affect the climate of the surrounding area. These schemes now seem impractical, even without consideration of the resulting salinization.

Mining the desert
In Australia, the only economic mineral that is directly associated with arid conditions is opal. Opal is formed by the precipitation of silica-bearing solutions near the Earth's surface,

which combine with salt from salt lakes. Coober Pedy in South Australia is a famous opal town, which has changed from a tiny settlement where the miners actually lived underground (to escape the heat), to a developed town with a water supply and many surface buildings.

Other mineral deposits have been found in the desert. These include gold, with major deposits in the Kalgoorlie area; lead and zinc, with major deposits at Broken Hill; copper and uranium at Olympic Dam; and iron ore at Mount Tom Price in Western Australia. These sites typify the largescale mineral finds, and demonstrate all the problems encountered by remote towns in deserts, such as water supply, communication, entertainment, education, and social relations.

▲ **A miner** is lowered into a shaft in an opal field near the South Australian outback town of Coober Pedy. Opals are an apt metaphor for the riches of the Australian desert. Each stone owes its delicate coloration to the presence of minute quantities of water. If an opal is allowed to dry out completely, it loses its colour, and its monetary value declines enormously.

Some mines are underground, but many are large openpit excavations. To the effects of mining should be added the disturbance caused by exploration (often by networks of vehicle tracks), and waste disposal. The mines have resulted in the establishment of an infrastructure of railroads, highways, and pipelines. Mining covers about half of one percent of Australia's land area, so its environmental impact is much less than agricultural or pastoral activities, or even urbanization. The potential environmental damage caused by various mining activities has forced all major mining companies to employ their own environmental officers. They are concerned with all aspects of mining, pollution, waste disposal, and reclamation. Mining companies face extremely close scrutiny and are expected to maintain high standards of environmental management. Both the federal and state governments have enacted legislation requiring the assessment of the environmental impact of new mining projects.

Another issue raised by mining operations is that of Aboriginal landrights. Only recently have Australian Aborigines been granted rights to land that is important to them for cultural and historical reasons. In the past, the discovery of potentially valuable mineral deposits in Aboriginal lands has resulted in massive relocation programs, often from culturally significant sites.

THE CHALLENGE OF CONSERVATION

Desert environments are highly sensitive and extremely susceptible to the effects of new usage. Local threats from mining, industry, and overgrazing worsen the problem enough, but major changes in the use of water and possible climatic change can cause even greater damage. What little life there is in deserts can be all too easily destroyed, and desert margins may become increasingly desertified as human activity ruins productive land. While some of these problems are global and must be addressed as such, others relate specifically to the use of particular desert areas. It is essential to formulate strategies for restricting damage and for ensuring the sustainable use of these harsh yet delicate environments.

The threat of desertification is real. As has been described earlier, it occurs when ecological processes and conditions characteristic of deserts extend into formerly semiarid areas. It is possible for this to happen in two major ways.

First, desertification can occur when there are major changes in climatic conditions. There have been such changes throughout geological history in a quite natural way. The most recent of these has been a steady warming of the Earth since the last ice age, which has in general brought wetter conditions. Today, however, there is the additional factor of the burning of fossil fuels, which, through the release of carbon dioxide, is generally considered to be leading to more rapid global warming. This could cause a shift in climatic belts, and possibly the expansion of some deserts, although it also might cause the contraction of others. There is considerable scientific debate over which of these effects might predominate, and what little evidence we have is at best confusing.

Second, it is widely believed that much recent desertification has been the result of human intervention—such as irrigation or overburdening land with livestock—although again there is much debate on the matter. Combined with a series of dry years, some human activities can indeed lead to desert-like conditions. This kind of desertification, however,

◀ **Signs of**
*desertification on
fields on the outskirts
of the city of Ségou,
Mali. The causes of
desertification in the
world's arid regions
vary greatly from place
to place. In some
regions desertification
is directly attributable
to human activity, in
other regions a gradual
change in climate has
created the problem.*

is not occurring along broad fronts. It is patchy, depending on local ecological conditions and human pressures. As a consequence, initiatives to solve these problems need to be targeted at a local level.

The fragile desert

The ecological systems of the deserts and their margins are delicately adjusted to the local conditions. Besides aridity, deserts experience great variations in rainfall, from day to day, month to month and year to year. They are also subject to extreme events of irregular occurrence, such as floods and fires. Desert ecologies are adapted to longterm variations in rainfall, which typically involve series of years with very low rainfall interspersed with rare years of relatively high rainfall during which the deserts bloom.

Despite this adaptability, and a resilience that allows desert margins to recover from prolonged dry periods, many desert ecosystems are sensitive to some kinds of human activity. Recovery from disturbance is constrained by the limited availability of moisture, which restricts plant growth and soil development. This means that disruption is difficult to reverse because, similarly, the ecosystems have so few resources for recovery.

Common misconceptions

The conservation needs of desert environments are poorly understood in comparison to issues such as rainforest depletion. There are two quite common misunderstandings about deserts and their margins. The first is that they are rarely exploited and therefore in a relatively pristine condition. The second is that, because they appear to be so barren of life, they have little diversity.

The truth is somewhat different. Deserts and their margins are important in the world's ecology for a number of reasons. They are extensive, covering about 30 percent of the Earth's surface, and diverse, with a variety of biological systems. They are home to a large number of people. Furthermore, they are often exploited.

The pressures that threaten to degrade and destroy desert ecosystems vary from place to place. Some of these pressures are local, such as population growth; others are the result of external pressures to exploit resources. The ability of deserts to cope with these pressures varies. Some human communities have the resources to invest in conservation. Other communities, with pressing problems related to poverty, cannot afford the time or money needed to invest in protecting natural resources for longterm use.

HUMAN IMPACTS

For many centuries, communities have survived and pros-pered in the deserts, despite periodic droughts and famines. Their success was based on ways of managing resources that were adjusted to the environment or were at very low intensity. They usually survived without destroying or seriously degrading the natural resources on which they relied. In recent decades, the situation has begun to change as a result of population growth, economic pressures, and political and social change.

Population growth

Today, many desert regions face rapidly growing popula-tions. This is partly a result of improved access to modern medical services, which has reduced infant mortality and improved maternal health. It is also a result of the continua-tion of traditional values that perceive children as a sign of economic strength and source of security in old age. Wealth from oil is another important factor.

In many deserts, the population is growing because of migration. In some cases, notably the United States and parts of the Middle East, migrants are moving to towns that have been developed to support industrial and mineral development. Rapid population growth in som deserts, especially in developing countries, increases the demands upon the regions' natural resources. This frequently leads to degradation, given the limited potential for increased out-put. Economic development itself puts ecological pressure on desert environments. Much of this pressure comes from the search for improved incomes by individuals as aspira-tions rise. This is reinforced by the demands of taxation and declining real prices for agricultural produce, which force farmers to increase their output and use natural resources more heavily in order to maintain their incomes. In addition, many governments frequently encourage the production of crops for export, so that they can finance imports or repay foreign debts.

A number of the ecological problems faced in deserts are caused by the ways in which governments treat indigenous people. Native Americans, the Aborigines of Australia and the nomadic pastoralists of Central Asia and the Sahara have all suffered at the hands of their governments. Their rights have been neglected and land has been taken (usually for development schemes from which they rarely benefit).

Resource conflicts and degradation

Pastoral people rely on their livestock, so that as the human population grows, so must the number of animals if stan-

▶ *A wodaabe nomad looks over her herd of cattle in Niger. The barren landscape looks devoid of much nutritional vegetation. It is the pressures brought on by development, rather than by traditional land uses, that brings on most degradation of grazing land.*

dards of living are not to fall. They have the additional problem that neighboring agricultural communities are also under pressure which drives them to exclude grazing from bigger and bigger areas. Taking land for irrigated agriculture removes yet more land from grazing. These restrictions occur most often on land that is critical to pastoralism in the dry-season: the wet pastures near the rivers.

Preserving pastoralism
In many regions, social change has led to the collapse of traditional range-management agreements, which in the past prevented overgrazing. Such social changes affect traditional society and reduce the effectiveness of the constraints that this imposed. There is increased competition for resources as populations grow and community structures are disrupted by state intervention. Absentee stock owners cause further problems because they tend to overburden their pastures.

The solutions to these problems vary. One approach is to recognize the right of pastoral societies, despite their lack of political power, and ensure that their traditional lands are not encroached upon. An integrated approach is required, with attention given to economic diversification, poverty alleviation, and increased economic security. In addition, pastoral communities have to re-establish pasture management systems that have in the past and can again ensure sustainable use of the existing resources.

EXPLOITATION AND DEVELOPMENT

Water is the scarcest commodity in the desert. Because demand usually exceeds supply, it is common for communities and their engineers to intervene in the natural hydrological (water) cycle. Irrigation water, for example, is usually drawn from underground sources that have accumulated over centuries or millennia. Some are recharged by rainfall in neighboring areas, but most came into existence in wetter times. If these water sources are used more rapidly than they are recharged, the cultivation that they support is unsustainable.

Desert soils contain salts of different kinds. When irrigation is poorly managed, excess water leads to the accumulation of salts in the upper layers of the soil, making the land infertile. Irrigation may also cause waterlogging. The problems of salinization and waterlogging are thought to affect over 30 percent of the irrigated land in deserts.

Economic change and urbanization

The ecological problems that face agricultural and pastoral desert communities today suggest that there is a need for economic diversification. The changes would reduce the pressures upon the resource base. There are no easy remedies, however, in the alternative economic activities that are being developed. Each has its own ecological problems.

▼ *A Berber woman from the Grand Atlas Mountain region of Morocco carries a large bundle of firewood back to her village. Increasing population places increasing pressure on the environment.*

Urbanization is one aspect of economic change and diversification. Urban dwellers, however, especially in poor countries, demand large amounts of fuelwood for cooking their food. So great is the demand for fuelwood that in some countries there is no woody vegetation remaining within a 60-mile (100-kilometer) radius of major urban centers. The need for wood rather than other sources of energy is partly a problem of poverty because, despite the long distances over which the wood must often be carried, it is still the cheapest fuel for the urban poor. The cutting of wood for fuel is not generally a problem in the rural areas of poor desert countries.

In the urban areas of the developed deserts the competition is not so much for woodfuel as for water to sustain high standards of living. The growth of towns in North America's Sun Belt, in response to the movement of high-technology industries and retired people to the dry and sunny environment, has led to enormous demands for water. In most cases, these have been met by using local groundwater supplies and by piping water from outside these regions

Minerals and cattle

Major mineral deposits are often found in desert regions, for instance, oil in the Middle East, uranium and iron ore in Australia, and diamonds in Namibia. The extraction of these minerals requires vast quantities of water and produces wastes, both of which can damage the fragile desert environment. The competition for water jeopardizes less high-value production, as in agriculture, and may severely deplete water supplies that are not renewable. In some cases as in the Goldfields of Western Australia, water is brought huge distances by pipeline.

Mining also creates some very toxic wastes. These may be carried short distances by water, and then deposited in noxious ponds, or they may rise up in dust lifted by the wind from mine dumps, as also in the goldfields of Western Australia. The massive copper mines in northern Chile, or the iron mines in other parts of Western Australia, create immense holes in the ground and great barren piles of waste surrounding them.

Economic diversification through modern cattle ranching is affecting the ecology of desert margins, including those of the Kalahari. To encourage commercial ranching, large farms have been established on what used to be communal grazing areas. The resulting pressure upon the remaining communal pasture causes overgrazing. Fences have also been established to keep out game and stop the mixing of cattle and game, which might spread cattle diseases, such as foot-and-mouth disease. In a number of cases these fences have severely disrupted the seasonal movement of game.

CONSERVING DESERTS

The deserts may at first seem to be in good condition: international assessments claim that about six percent of their area is damaged. The assessments themselves make many caveats, the principal one being that they have poor information about many deserts. This is not surprising, given the enormous data hole that many deserts fall into, and may not be so alarming, if we agree that the least known deserts are probably also the least damaged. A more worrying caveat is that damage statistics given by area are not the only ones that matter in an environment where many people and wildlife are very mobile. Very large numbers of migratory birds are threatened when their habitats, like the Mesopotamian marshes in Iraq, are drained. The migratory Houbara bustard, and the oryx are known to be close to extinction because of migratory hunters.

Assessing future needs
Treating deserts as a whole, moreover, is in danger of losing sight of the fact that the areas that are damaged are the ones where most people live. These are the areas, like the environs of the Aral Sea, or the ends of irrigation canals in Pakistan, where livelihoods, even lives, are in real danger. Neither do figures on the proportion of the deserts that is damaged pick up the siltation of reservoirs that is threatening so many irrigation schemes, or the exhaustion of deep aquifers of fossil water that is also happening in many countries. Moreover, none of these measures allows us to look forward to a worrying future under climate change, which almost everyone agrees is now happening, and a large majority of scientists believe will continue. Here again, although predictions of climate change show that the deserts may not suffer to nearly the extent, say, of the polar regions (although the deserts of southern Africa may suffer quite severely), the main concerns are not these most obvious ones. The deserts that are watered by rivers fed by snow- and glacier-melt may have been seeing an increase in their water supply as the melting first accelerates, but when the glaciers reach closer to total local extinction, they will suffer very severely. The deserts round the South American mountains are already seeing smaller flows; the deserts round the mountain massifs in Central Asia (in Pakistan; Afghanistan, the central Asian Republics of the former Soviet Union, and China) will almost certainly feel the pinch in the near future.

Growth in population, once thought to be one of the big global environmental concerns, can now be seen to hold hidden opportunities as well as dangers. The dangers come in the next one or two decades when population will almost

certainly continue to rise in the deserts of the developing world. This will put pressure on resources, particularly of water, and may lead to unemployment, and so to more poverty and then to dissatisfaction, and in turn to political unrest, perhaps even terrorism. But, the developed world is rapidly running out of labor, and this may mean one of two more positive things. Either labor-intensive industries will migrate to the places where the labor is (although deserts, with their unreliable water supplies are unlikely to receive much from this source); or the labor will migrate to work in the burgeoning service sector in countries where the reproduction of labor is pitifully low, and then send home remittances. The total sum of remittances to the developing world has been running at a very much higher level than international aid for some years, and there is no reason to think that the flow will not continue, even increase as the developed world realizes its need for labor. Remittances usually mean more investment at home.

The story is rather different in the deserts of the developed world. Their future seems to be in retirement, recreation, and tourism. These developments hold their own

▲ *The once common* nomadic lifestyle of the people of the northern Sahel is increasingly becoming an exception rather than the rule.

dangers. The retirement centers in places like Palm Springs in the California desert consume vast amounts of water (on golf courses and attempts at producing gardens like those in wetter climates), and as aquifers empty and the competition for scarcer water intensifies these may be threatened.

Halting land degredation

Land degradation is a large item in the global agenda. The arid parts of the deserts (but not the hyperarid cores) and the desert margins have their own international organization to cover land degradation (the UNCCD—the United Nations Convention to Combat Desertification). It is mandated to ensure that all countries remotely connected with deserts produce a plan to combat land degradation, and has in place programs to ensure popular participation in anti-degradation measures. There is no doubt that there is land degradation in arid and hyperarid deserts: huge areas of land have undoubt-

edly suffered from salinization in Iraq, Pakistan, and Central Asia, and statistics show that the problem is expanding fast in China and the United States (to mention only some deserts). Some of the damage is thousands of years old, and most of that has not yet been rectified. The worst example of the baleful results of irrigation is the Aral Sea, which began to contract after a large proportion of the water in the two main feeder rivers was diverted to irrigated cotton in the 1960s and 1970s. By 1987 its level had fallen 46 feet (14 meters); its salt concentration had doubled from about 10 grams/liter in 1961 to 40 grams/liter in 1994; 20 of the 24 native fish species had been lost and there was a virtual end of commercial fishery; dust storms became toxic with salts and agricultural pesticides; 97 percent of women in the surrounding area are now anaemic; life expectancy is significantly lower than in surrounding areas.

Salinization

The remedy for salinization is well known, but expensive, and very much more so when it has to be applied retrospectively, than it is to apply before the problem escalates (which is rarely done). The remedy is first to ensure that the water table in the soil is kept below the capillary fringe (the depth over which water can be drawn to the surface by capillarity), and this requires either deep tube wells to enable the water table to be lowered by pumping water to the surface, or deep drains to take it away. After some drainage system is in place, enough water should be applied at the surface of the soil to wash salts out. The expenses do not end with these already expensive measures. The saline water that is pumped up or drained away is often too saline to re-use, and may have to be lead away in special canals to the sea or to special reservoirs where it can evaporate. The capital and maintenance costs of drainage are vast; let alone the disruption of livelihoods that is involved in building the drains. Most governments quail at the costs. On the Colorado River in the western United States, an even more expensive strategy has been adopted: to desalinate the water that crosses the border in Mexico to a level of salinity that accords with an international agreement. $1 billion was set aside by Congress for the project, but has yet to be spent. The environmental costs of salinization on the Colorado, as on other rivers, are also huge: damaged wetlands, damaged populations of fish, damaged riparian habitats, and damaged seas.

Desert soils do not generally suffer accelerated erosion. There is very little agriculture outside the irrigated areas, and that agriculture has a very small impact on rates of erosion; the damage erosion does to their productivity is almost

▼ *A large water hazard* *lies along the 16th* *fairway of the Desert* *Springs Palm Course in* *Palm Desert, California.* *As water resources* *become increasingly* *scarce, the recreational* *and tourist industries will* *come into conflict with* *local farmers.*

impossible to measure, given that their productivity fluctuates wildly with rainfall. There may be damage to rangelands, but here too, the general belief is that variations in the productivity of desert pastures are much more determined by rainfall (about which, climate change aside, little can be done) than by grazing (except the few areas where stock are concentrated, such as around wells).

Deserts do indeed produce most of the dust that blows around the world, but little can be done about that either, short of asphalting over many thousands of square yards of desert. The water for plantations in the dustiest areas is hundreds of miles away on the desert margins, and is already spoken for by irrigation, domestic, and industrial use. Moreover many agricultural and forestry operations on the peripheries of deserts depend on the nutrients that come with the dust, to say nothing of the oceans, where dust may bolster the capability to fix carbon. There is, for all that, one set of desert dust sources that should and could be controlled: the dust that comes from desiccated lakes like the Aral Sea and Owens Lake in California. Sources of dust like unpaved roads and dryland farming in semiarid areas may not figure large as global sources of dust, but they can be controlled by asphalt or by regulations on plowing, which would considerably mitigate local nuisance dust.

Sustainable desert development

Sustainability is a laudable aim, but what could it mean in an environment like the desert, where rainfall fluctuates hugely at a great range of scales: wet and dry days; wet and dry places a few hundred yards apart; wet and dry years, decades, centuries ...; and one that is threatened with almost inevitable climate change? The response of most desert people has always been take it while you can, before, for example, the grass withers and dies. There are good scientific reasons for applauding this strategy. Little damage is probably done in this way, unless enough seeds are prevented from germinating after the next shower, or unless the forage is taken out of the mouths of endangered wildlife. The strategy is, after all, also that of most desert animals themselves.

If sustainability is defined, as it most commonly, is as: "development that meets the needs of the present without compromising the ability of future generations to meet their own needs," there are problems, for almost all development compromises the future in some way. In this situation, policies for sustainable development must make a tricky judgment: what degree of damage to allow? The "hard" sustainable lobby would allow no development at all, for

▶ *An open-cast copper mine near Salt Lake City, Utah. Stripped down to bare rock, the bleak slopes and terraces will take many years to grow even sparse vegetation. Among the many other forms of environmental damage caused by such mining activity is the creation of large amounts of metal-rich dust that can poison the surrounding landscape.*

example of tourist hotels (which undoubtedly have been competing for scarce and unrenewable water), or black-topped roads (which undoubtedly disturb desert wildlife).

The realist calls for caution in these developments, and this policy has been called "sensible sustainability," which, sensible as it is, is the much harder path to follow. Part of sensible sustainability, the IUCN (International Union for the Conservation of Nature) believes, is to involve local people in conserving their resources, a process that has been called "community involvement." There are pilot schemes for this with the Peruvian desert vicuña and among Bedouin in Syria, and many other areas. But community conservation also has its dangers: the community often chooses development that the experts see as unsustainable. Nonetheless, community conservation is the way forward, if cautiously followed. Another great hope amongst conservationists has been "ecotourism," and at its best this too has a great future in deserts. At its worst it attracts tourists to very dubiously "ecological" tours, which can still do great damage to the environment.

GLOSSARY

Words followed by an asterisk * have their own entries

aestivation Seasonal state of torpor during the hot months of the year. Animals undergo aestivation to survive harsh summers for many of the same reasons as some animals undergo hibernation in winter.

alluvial fan Cone-shaped sediment created by deposition from a desert river, whose apex is at the point where the river leaves the mountains.

alluvium Fine sediment deposited by a river. The sediment consists largely of mud, sand and gravel, is often highly fertile and supports agriculture.

anticyclone Another name for a high-pressure zone*.

aquifer Layer of porous rock that contains large quantities of water.

arid Describing climates or regions with an average annual rainfall of less than 8 inches (200 millimeters).

badlands Desert region that is dissected by dense networks of rills and deep, steep-sided gullies and is devoid of vegetation. Erosion in badlands is rapid.

barchan Another name for a crescent dune*.

biodiversity Number and variety of plant and animal species in a given region.

biome Largest type of ecological community that is generally identifiable as distinct, for example, tundra, savanna, temperate woodland, rain forest, or desert.

carrying capacity Maximum number of grazing animals that a given area of pastoral land can sustain without degradation through overgrazing or other problems.

catch-crop Products of opportunist crop farming. Such crops are grown only at times when rainfall is sufficient.

continentality Conditions and effects of a continental climate. Such a climate is one that is not affected by maritime influences because it occurs in the central regions of a vast landmass. It lacks moisture and has pronounced differences in temperature between summer and winter.

crescent dune Crescent-or horseshoe-shaped dune. Such dunes are relatively rare but are noted for their speed of movement. (Also known as a barchan*).

deflation Removal of loose surface material by the wind.

desert pavement Dense layer of stones on top of a desert soil, formed in many ways, among which are deflation* and water-erosion.

desert varnish Dark, surface sheen that is found on the surface of many desert rock outcrops. The colour derives from iron and manganese, some derived from the rock beneath, but mostly coming from dust. Lichens and bacteria help to fix these elements. (Also known as rock varnish.)

drought Period during which rainfall does not reach expected levels in a given region.

dust devil Small, but powerful whirlwind that picks up dust, sand and other loose surface material.

ecosystem Relationships between the members of a community of plants and animals, and the interactions of that community with its physical environment.

environment Physical and biological factors that characterize a certain area with respect to the life in that area, or the set of such factors that affect on organism or species.

enzyme Biological catalyst, that is, a substance in an organism that increases the rate at which chemical reactions take place within the organism. Enzymes, which are proteins, are essential to life because most important reactions would take place far too slowly without them.

erosion Wearing away of soil and rock by the action of wind or water.

evaporite Substance that, having been dissolved in a liquid, is left behind when the liquid evaporates. Salt left on the bottom of a dry lake, for example, is an evaporite.

flash flood Brief torrent of water, usually caused by a heavy rainstorm, that occurs especially in deserts.

floodplain Flat land bordering a river that consists of alluvium* that has been deposited by the river.

fossil water Water that entered an aquifer* many thousands of years ago, when the climate was wetter than it is now. Fossil water is not being renewed by present rainfall.

groundwater Water in an aquifer*.

Hadley Cell Circulation of air in which hot, moist air rises at the Equator (where the moisture is released as rain), moves polewards to a latitude of about 30°, and then cools and sinks, flowing back towards the Equator.

high-pressure zone Weather system with high atmospheric pressure in which air sinks, diverges outwards and disperses cloud. (Also known as an anticyclone.)

hyperarid Describing climates or regions with an average annual rainfall of less than 1 inch (25 millimeters).

ice age Any one of a number of periods in the Earth's geological past when glaciers spread to cover much more of the Earth's surface than they do usually. The last ice age reached its maximum about 20,000 years ago and ended (fitfully) about 8,000 years ago.

infrared Part of the electromagnetic spectrum (which includes radio waves, microwaves, visible light, and suchlike) of slightly longer wavelength than red light, and invisible to the human eye.

inselberg Isolated, steep-sided hill, usually found protruding from semiarid plains.

intermontane Area that lies between mountain ranges.

isohiyet Line on a rainfall map that joins together points that have the same rainfall.

linear dune Long, sinuous dune that is fairly straight overall. Such dunes are the most common type and may reach several miles in length. (Also known as a *sayf**)

loess Accumulation of dust particles deposited by the wind.

metabolic rate Rate at which the internal chemical processes, and thus many of the functions, of a living organism proceed.

petrochemical industry Any industry involved in the exploitation of crude oil, natural gas, and their derivatives. For example, the processing of crude oil into its constituent factions, or the manufacture of plastics from petroleum.

photosynthesis Process by which plants form carbohydrates from carbon dioxide and water using the energy of sunlight. Plants use the carbohydrates for various purposes, but especially as a source of energy.

potash Common name for a number of potassium-containing compounds. The majority of mined potash is used in the manufacture of fertilizers, although it has many other uses in the chemical industry.

precipitation In meteorology, moisture in the atmosphere condensing and, generally, falling to Earth as rain, dew, hail, sleet, or snow.

qanat Artificial tunnel dug to carry water from a well, usually high up on an alluvial fan* to a settlement or oasis further down the fan. The term qanat is used in Iran and Pakistan. Other names are used in Arabia and North Africa.

rangeland Land that has vegetation suitable for grazing livestock.

renewable resource Any resource that is not diminished when it is used or else replenishes itself very rapidly. For example, the use of sunlight in a photoelectric cell does not diminish the supply of sunlight. On the other hand, resources of oil will, in effect, never replenish themselves.

rock varnish Another name for desert varnish*.

runoff Surface water (usually from rainfall) moving over land, as opposed to being absorbed into the ground.

salinization Increased levels of salt brought about by a variety of processes involving the evaporation of water.

saltation Jumping motion of sand particles that are being moved by the wind.

salt flat/salt pan The residue of salts left behind on the ground when a lake evaporates

sand Fragments of rock with a particle size of between 0.008 and 0.08 inches (0.2 and 2 millimeters). Particles smaller than this are generally referred to as dust, although the distinction is not formal.

sayf Another name for a linear dune*.

semiarid Describing climates or regions with an average annual rainfall of less than 24 inches (600 millimeters).

stratum Any one of the distinct layers into which sedimentary rocks are divided. Each layer corresponds to a particular period of sedimentation.

succulent Any of a large group of flowering plants with thick, fleshy stems and leaves. The plants are adapted for arid climates and include the cacti.

sustainable Describing a method of agriculture, way of life, power-production process or similar that can be maintained indefinitely. Sustainable agriculture, for example, involves such things as farming practices that do not degrade the land, and do not consume non-renewable water supplies.

wadi Arabic term for a river channel, generally one that flows only intermittently.

water table Level in the ground below which rock strata or soils are saturated with water.

weathering Breakdown of rocks resulting from a number of processes including freezing and thawing, heating and cooling, wetting and drying, the expansion of salts as they crystallize, biological activity and solution by percolating water.

yardang Elongated hillock of rock that has been formed by the action of the wind.

CREDITS

INDEX